YouTube
Mastery

First
Edition
2024

by R.H Rizvi

WELCOME TO YOUTUBE MASTERY 2024 UNVEILING THE SECRETS OF SUCCESS"!

I'M ECSTATIC THAT YOU'RE STARTING THIS JOURNEY TOWARDS YOUTUBE EXPERTISE. THIS BOOK IS YOUR ALL-INCLUSIVE GUIDE TO CONQUERING THE ART OF CREATING A SUCCESSFUL CHANNEL, MAXIMIZING THE POTENTIAL OF THE BIGGEST VIDEO-SHARING PLATFORM WORLDWIDE, AND NAVIGATING THE EVER-CHANGING WORLD OF CONTENT CREATION.

"YOUTUBE MASTERY 2024" IS MEANT TO GIVE YOU USEFUL INSIGHTS, USEFUL ADVICE, AND THE MOST RECENT TRENDS INFLUENCING THE FUTURE OF YOUTUBE, REGARDLESS OF WHETHER YOU'RE AN EXPERIENCED VIDEO CREATOR TRYING TO HONE YOUR TECHNIQUES OR A NOVICE HOPING TO LEAVE YOUR MARK.

PREPARE TO LEARN ABOUT EVERYTHING FROM CREATING CONTENT AND ENGAGING AUDIENCES TO MONETIZATION TECHNIQUES AND STAYING AHEAD OF THE EVER CHANGING DIGITAL MARKET.

I'M THRILLED TO BE YOUR MENTOR ON THIS INSPIRING TRIP AS YOU EMBARK ON YOUR PATH TO YOUTUBE MASTERY.

TOGETHER, WE WILL EXPLORE THE KEYS TO ENHANCING YOUR YOUTUBE PROFILE AND TURNING YOUR ARTISTIC PURSUITS INTO A RELIABLE SOURCE OF INCOME.

HAPPY CREATING!

[R.H RIZVI]
AUTHOR, "YOUTUBE MASTERY 2024: UNVEILING THE SECRETS OF SUCCESS"

TABLE OF CONTENTS

INTRODUCTION
UNLOCKING THE SECRETS TO YOUTUBE SUCCESS

WITHIN THE EVER CHANGING FIELD OF ONLINE CONTENT CREATION, YOUTUBE IS A DOMINANT PLATFORM THAT PROVIDES COUNTLESS CHANCES FOR PEOPLE TO CONTRIBUTE INSIGHTFUL INFORMATION, DEVELOP VIBRANT COMMUNITIES, AND EXHIBIT THEIR SKILLS. THE ALL-INCLUSIVE GUIDE "YOUTUBE MASTERY 2024 FIRST EDITION" WILL HELP YOU NAVIGATE THIS EVER-CHANGING DOMAIN, DISCOVER THE KEYS TO YOUTUBE SUCCESS, AND ESTABLISH YOURSELF AS A SIGNIFICANT AND INFLUENTIAL CONTENT CREATOR.

CHAPTER 1
THE YOUTUBE LANDSCAPE UNVEILED

NAVIGATING THE DIGITAL CANVAS

GREETINGS FROM "THE YOUTUBE LANDSCAPE UNVEILED" FIRST CHAPTER. WE'LL GO THROUGH THE LAYERS OF YOUTUBE'S DIGITAL CANVAS TO UNCOVER THE COMPLEX ENVIRONMENT THAT HAS ENTHRALLED VIEWERS ALL AROUND THE WORLD. THIS CHAPTER IS YOUR STARTING POINT FOR LEARNING ABOUT THE HISTORY OF THE PLATFORM, ITS INFLUENCE, AND THE VARIETY OF INFORMATION THAT EXISTS ON IT AND HELPS TO SHAPE THE DIGITAL WORLD.

THE GENESIS OF YOUTUBE

LET'S GO BACK TO YOUTUBE'S EARLY DAYS TO BEGIN OUR JOURNEY. THIS PLATFORM WAS CREATED IN 2005 TO GIVE PEOPLE A PLACE TO SHARE THEIR MOMENTS, STORIES, AND CREATIVE ENDEAVORS WITH A WORLDWIDE AUDIENCE. THE CREATORS' STRAIGHTFORWARD YET INNOVATIVE IDEA WAS TO DEMOCRATIZE THE PRODUCTION AND CONSUMPTION OF VIDEO CONTENT.

CULTURAL AND GLOBAL IMPACT

SINCE ITS LAUNCH, YOUTUBE HAS HAD A SIGNIFICANT CULTURAL IMPACT ON PEOPLE ALL ACROSS THE WORLD, EXTENDING BEYOND ITS DIGITAL FOUNDATIONS. WITH ITS ABILITY TO CREATE VIRAL SENSATIONS THAT BRING PEOPLE TOGETHER AND SPARK SOCIAL AND POLITICAL DEBATES, YOUTUBE HAS GROWN TO BE A POWERFUL FORCE INFLUENCING HOW WE VIEW AND ENGAGE WITH THE WORLD.

DIVERSE CONTENT ECOSYSTEM

A RICH AND VARIED CONTENT ECOSYSTEM IS THE BEATING HEART OF YOUTUBE. DISCOVER THE WIDE RANGE OF CONTENT GENRES, FROM ENTERTAINMENT AND INFORMATIVE FILMS TO SPECIALIZED HOBBIES AND SUBCULTURES. ARTISTS USE A WIDE RANGE OF COLORS TO CREATE WORKS ON THIS CANVAS, SO THERE IS SOMETHING FOR EVERYONE.

AUDIENCE ENGAGEMENT AND COMMUNITY DYNAMICS

YOUTUBE IS A VIBRANT COMMUNITY AS WELL AS A PLATFORM. EXPLORE THE SYMBIOTIC TIES THAT ARISE BETWEEN PRODUCERS AND VIEWERS THROUGH THE INTRICACIES OF AUDIENCE ENGAGEMENT. LIKES, SHARES, AND COMMENTS COMBINE TO FORM THE FOUNDATION OF AN ONLINE COMMUNITY THAT KNOWS NO GEOGRAPHICAL BOUNDS.

EVOLUTION OF CONTENT CREATION

Observe the development of YouTube content creation. Artists have always pushed the limits of inventiveness, from the early days of grainy webcam videos to the polished productions of today. The evolution shows the development of a global creative community in addition to technological improvements.

THE RISE OF INFLUENCERS AND DIGITAL ENTREPRENEURS

This chapter will examine the emergence of digital entrepreneurs and influencers who have made their passion their career. Recognize the tactics that propelled users to fame and made YouTube a platform for successful business ventures and career launches.

IMPACT ON TRADITIONAL MEDIA

YouTube has upended the landscape of traditional media by questioning accepted wisdom and giving a voice to a variety of viewpoints. Examine the ways in which the digital revolution has affected conventional media and ushered in a new period of entertainment and storytelling.

YOUTUBE AS AN EDUCATIONAL HUB

YouTube has developed into a global center for education in addition to entertainment. Discover how the platform has developed into an informal yet effective source of knowledge for learners worldwide, offering anything from skill-building content to courses on a variety of subjects.

NAVIGATING YOUTUBE'S INTERFACE

We'll walk you through the UI if this is your first time using YouTube's digital platform. To ensure you get the most out of your YouTube experience, familiarize yourself with the features, functionality, and tools that are available to both creators and viewers.

THE INFLUENCE OF YOUTUBE ON POP CULTURE

Examine YouTube's significant impact on popular culture. See how YouTube has shaped trends and given rise to a platform for cultural expression, impacting how we define and express ourselves and become a vital component of the cultural zeitgeist.

THE DARK AND BRIGHT SIDES OF YOUTUBE

RECOGNIZE YOUTUBE'S CONTRADICTIONS, BOTH ITS ADVANTAGES AND DISADVANTAGES. IT DEALS WITH ISSUES LIKE FALSE INFORMATION AND CONTENT DISPUTES EVEN AS IT ENCOURAGES CREATIVITY AND COMMUNITY. GET A COMPREHENSIVE GRASP OF THE DUAL NATURE OF THE PLATFORM.

YOUTUBE'S ROLE IN SOCIAL MOVEMENTS

YOUTUBE SERVES AS A STAGE FOR SOCIAL MOVEMENTS IN ADDITION TO BEING A PLATFORM FOR PLEASURE. EXAMINE THE WAYS IN WHICH IT HAS CONTRIBUTED TO THE ADVANCEMENT OF SOCIAL CAUSES, RAISED AWARENESS, AND INSPIRED COMMUNITY ACTION FOR CHANGE.

THE FUTURE OF YOUTUBE

AS WE WRAP OUT THIS CHAPTER, TAKE A LOOK AT YOUTUBE'S FUTURE. LEARN ABOUT NEW TRENDS AND TECHNOLOGY DEVELOPMENTS AS WELL AS YOUTUBE'S LIKELY FUTURE COURSE TO REMAIN AHEAD OF THE ALWAYS CHANGING DIGITAL LANDSCAPE.

CONCLUSION CHAPTER 1
EMBARKING ON A DIGITAL ODYSSEY

YOU'VE STARTED YOUR DIGITAL JOURNEY AROUND YOUTUBE'S WIDE WORLD WITH THIS INTRODUCTION CHAPTER. I HOPE YOU GAIN A DEEPER GRASP OF THIS DIGITAL CANVAS AS WE CONTINUE TO UNCOVER ADDITIONAL LAYERS IN THE UPCOMING CHAPTERS. I ALSO HOPE YOU FIND INSPIRATION TO EXPLORE AND ADD TO THE DIVERSE LANDSCAPE THAT IS YOUTUBE. GREETINGS ON THIS VOYAGE!

CHAPTER 2
CRAFTING YOUR UNIQUE CHANNEL IDENTITY

THE ARTISTRY OF CHANNEL BRANDING

GREETINGS AND WELCOME TO "THE YOUTUBE LANDSCAPE UNVEILED," CHAPTER TWO. WE SET OFF ON A DIGITAL SELF-DISCOVERY QUEST IN THIS SEGMENT. "CRAFTING YOUR UNIQUE CHANNEL IDENTITY" EXPLORES THE RELEVANCE OF STANDING OUT IN THE LARGE SEA OF CONTENT AND BUILDING A CHANNEL THAT TRULY CONNECTS WITH YOUR AUDIENCE, ADDRESSING THE ARTISTRY BEHIND CHANNEL BRANDING.

DEFINING YOUR NICHE

CHOOSING YOUR SPECIALIZATION IS THE FIRST STEP IN CREATING A DISTINCTIVE CHANNEL. LEARN HOW TO FOCUS ON A PARTICULAR THEME OR AREA OF KNOWLEDGE THAT CORRESPONDS WITH YOUR PASSION AND AREA OF SKILL. THIS CHAPTER WALKS YOU THROUGH THE PROCESS OF CHOOSING A NICHE THAT APPEALS TO BOTH YOU AND YOUR INTENDED MARKET.

DEVELOPING A DISTINCT BRAND

A SUCCESSFUL CHANNEL REVOLVES AROUND A UNIQUE BRAND. EXPLORE THE NUANCES OF BRAND DEVELOPMENT, FROM CREATING VISUALLY APPEALING CONTENT AND PICKING A DISTINCTIVE CHANNEL NAME TO DEFINING A UNIFIED TONE AND STYLE. DISCOVER HOW TO BUILD A BRAND THAT CAPTIVATES AUDIENCES AND ENCOURAGES RECOGNITION.

UNDERSTANDING YOUR TARGET AUDIENCE

IT'S CRITICAL TO COMPREHEND YOUR TARGET AUDIENCE IN ORDER TO CREATE A CHANNEL IDENTITY THAT APPEALS TO THEM. EXAMINE METHODS FOR LOCATING AND ESTABLISHING A CONNECTION WITH YOUR IDEAL AUDIENCE. LEARN THINGS LIKE AUDIENCE PREFERENCES AND DEMOGRAPHICS TO HELP YOU CREATE AND IMPLEMENT ENGAGEMENT AND CONTENT STRATEGIES.

CRAFTING COMPELLING CHANNEL ART

ONE EFFECTIVE TECHNIQUE FOR CHANNEL BRANDING IS VISUAL APPEAL. LEARN HOW TO CREATE EYE-CATCHING CHANNEL ART, SUCH AS A BANNER THAT GRABS ATTENTION AND A UNIQUE LOGO. DISCOVER DESIGN CONCEPTS THAT WILL IMPROVE THE AESTHETICS OF YOUR CHANNEL AND HELP CREATE A VISUALLY UNIFIED BRAND IMAGE.

ESTABLISHING A CONSISTENT TONE AND STYLE

ESTABLISHING RECOGNITION AND TRUST REQUIRES CONSISTENCY. EXAMINE THE SIGNIFICANCE OF MAINTAINING A UNIFIED TONE AND AESTHETIC THROUGHOUT YOUR VIDEOS. MAINTAINING CONSISTENCY IN YOUR CONTENT DELIVERY, EDITING APPROACH, AND ON-SCREEN DEMEANOR FOSTERS A FEELING OF FAMILIARITY AND FAMILIARITY AMONG YOUR VIEWERS.

CREATING AN IMPACTFUL CHANNEL TRAILER

THE DIGITAL EQUIVALENT OF A FIRST IMPRESSION IS YOUR CHANNEL TRAILER. DEVELOP YOUR ABILITY TO PRODUCE A COMPELLING CHANNEL TRAILER THAT DRAWS IN NEW VIEWERS AND MOTIVATES THEM TO SUBSCRIBE. EXAMINE INTERACTION TACTICS AND STORYTELLING APPROACHES TO CREATE A TRAILER THAT ENTICES VIEWERS TO CHECK OUT MORE OF YOUR CHANNEL.

LEVERAGING UNIQUE SELLING POINTS

WHAT DISTINGUISHES YOUR CHANNEL FROM OTHERS? RECOGNIZE AND CAPITALIZE ON YOUR USPS TO MAKE A NAME FOR YOURSELF IN THE CONGESTED ONLINE MARKET. THIS CHAPTER HELPS YOU HIGHLIGHT THE UNIQUE QUALITIES OF YOUR CHANNEL, WHETHER IT'S YOUR EXPERIENCE, A UNIQUE FORMAT, OR A PARTICULAR STYLE.

BUILDING A MEMORABLE CHANNEL URL

A MEMORABLE CHANNEL URL GIVES YOUR BRANDING A MORE POLISHED LOOK. DISCOVER HOW TO ALTER THE URL OF YOUR CHANNEL TO MAKE IT EASIER TO REMEMBER AND SHARE. RECOGNIZE HOW IMPORTANT A SHORT, BRANDED URL IS TO IMPROVING THE ONLINE VISIBILITY AND ACCESSIBILITY OF YOUR CHANNEL.

UTILIZING THUMBNAILS EFFECTIVELY

YOUR WORK CAN BE ACCESSED VISUALLY THROUGH THUMBNAILS. LEARN HOW TO MAKE VISUALLY APPEALING THUMBNAILS THAT MAKE PEOPLE WANT TO CLICK. THIS CHAPTER PROVIDES YOU WITH THE TOOLS TO OPTIMIZE YOUR THUMBNAILS FOR MAXIMUM EFFECT, FROM DESIGN PRINCIPLES TO THE STRATEGIC USE OF TEXT AND GRAPHICS.

ENGAGING CHANNEL DESCRIPTIONS AND ABOUT SECTION

THE SPACE IN YOUR ABOUT AND CHANNEL DESCRIPTIONS IS CRUCIAL FOR BUILDING RELATIONSHIPS WITH YOUR VIEWERS. EXAMINE SUCCESSFUL METHODS FOR CREATING DESCRIPTIONS THAT ARE INTERESTING TO READ AND THAT REVEAL SOMETHING ABOUT YOUR PERSONALITY AND CONTENT. DISCOVER HOW TO CREATE A FEELING OF CONNECTION AND COMMUNITY BY UTILIZING THESE COMPONENTS.

SHOWCASING PLAYLISTS FOR CONTENT ORGANIZATION

PLAYLISTING YOUR MATERIAL IMPROVES THE VIEWING EXPERIENCE AND MAINTAINS AUDIENCE INTEREST. THIS CHAPTER WALKS YOU THROUGH THE PROCESS OF ORGANIZING PLAYLISTS SO THEY BEST PRESENT YOUR MATERIAL. DISCOVER HOW PLAYLISTS MAY MAKE FOR A SMOOTH AND ENTERTAINING VIEWING EXPERIENCE, FROM THEMATIC GROUPINGS TO THOUGHTFUL ARRANGING.

ENCOURAGING BRAND INTERACTION

ENCOURAGE COMMUNICATION AND INVOLVEMENT WITH YOUR BRAND. EXAMINE METHODS FOR GETTING VIEWERS TO ENGAGE WITH ONE ANOTHER BY LEAVING COMMENTS, LIKING, AND SHARING CONTENT. RECOGNIZE HOW CRUCIAL IT IS TO REPLY TO COMMENTS AND FOSTER A SENSE OF COMMUNITY THAT STRENGTHENS THE IDENTITY OF YOUR CHANNEL.

MONITORING AND ADAPTING YOUR BRAND STRATEGY

A DYNAMIC AND FLEXIBLE BRAND STRATEGY IS ESSENTIAL FOR SUCCESS. DISCOVER HOW TO TRACK THE EFFECTIVENESS OF YOUR CHANNEL BRANDING AND MAKE ANY CORRECTIONS. INVESTIGATE AUDIENCE FEEDBACK AND ANALYTICS TOOLS TO CONTINUOUSLY IMPROVE YOUR BRAND STRATEGY FOR MAXIMUM IMPACT AND RESONANCE.

CONCLUSION CHAPTER 2 YOUR CHANNEL, YOUR CANVAS

REMEMBER, AS WE WRAP UP THIS CHAPTER, THAT YOUR CHANNEL IS A DIGITAL CANVAS JUST BEGGING TO BE CUSTOMIZED WITH YOUR DISTINCT PERSONALITY. CREATE IT WITH SINCERITY, PURPOSE, AND A THOROUGH COMPREHENSION OF YOUR TARGET AUDIENCE. I HOPE THAT MY INVESTIGATION INTO CHANNEL BRANDING WILL MOTIVATE YOU TO DESIGN A DIGITAL ENVIRONMENT THAT NOT ONLY SHOWCASES YOUR ENTHUSIASM BUT ALSO DEEPLY CONNECTS WITH VIEWERS. HAPPY CREATING!

CHAPTER 3
CONTENT STRATEGY FOR IMPACTFUL VIDEOS

THE ART AND SCIENCE OF CAPTIVATING CONTENT

GREETINGS FROM CHAPTER 3 OF "THE YOUTUBE LANDSCAPE UNVEILED." WE EXPLORE YOUTUBE'S CONTENT, WHICH IS ITS CORE, IN THIS SECTION. THE ART AND SCIENCE OF MAKING VIDEOS THAT NOT ONLY GRAB VIEWERS' ATTENTION BUT ALSO HAVE A LASTING EFFECT ON THEM ARE EXAMINED IN "CONTENT STRATEGY FOR IMPACTFUL VIDEOS". THIS CHAPTER SERVES AS YOUR MANUAL FOR CREATING ENGAGING CONTENT, FROM CONCEPTION TO IMPLEMENTATION.

UNDERSTANDING YOUR AUDIENCE'S NEEDS AND PREFERENCES

KNOWING YOUR AUDIENCE IS THE FIRST STEP TOWARDS CREATING CONTENT THAT HAS AN IMPACT. EXAMINE STRATEGIES FOR DETERMINING YOUR AUDIENCE'S REQUIREMENTS, INCLINATIONS, AND EXPECTATIONS. LEARN THINGS LIKE VISITOR DEMOGRAPHICS AND ENGAGEMENT DATA TO HELP GUIDE YOUR CONTENT CREATION PROCESS.

DEFINING YOUR CONTENT VALUE PROPOSITION

IN ORDER TO DRAW IN AND KEEP VIEWERS, A STRONG VALUE PROPOSITION MUST BE CREATED. SUMMARIZE THE SPECIAL BENEFITS THAT YOUR AUDIENCE CAN RECEIVE FROM YOUR MATERIAL. THIS CHAPTER WILL ASSIST YOU IN DEFINING WHAT MAKES YOUR MATERIAL UNIQUE AND WORTHWHILE, WHETHER IT BE ENTERTAINMENT, EDUCATION, INSPIRATION, OR A MIX OF THESE.

CHOOSING CONTENT THEMES AND TOPICS

LOOK THROUGH THE WIDE RANGE OF THEMES AND TOPICS AVAILABLE FOR CONTENT TO SEE WHAT APPEALS TO YOUR VIEWERS AND FITS WITH THE IDENTITY OF YOUR CHANNEL. LEARN TECHNIQUES FOR COMING UP WITH IDEAS, LOOKING INTO TRENDS, AND CHOOSING SUBJECTS THAT WILL INTEREST YOU AND KEEP YOUR AUDIENCE INTERESTED.

CRAFTING CLICK-WORTHY TITLES AND THUMBNAILS

YOUR VIDEO'S TITLES AND THUMBNAILS SERVE AS THEIR ONLINE SHOP. DISCOVER HOW TO CREATE CAPTIVATING, SEARCH-FRIENDLY TITLES THAT WILL GET READERS TO CLICK. DISCOVER DESIGN IDEAS AND TECHNIQUES FOR PRODUCING ATTENTION-GRABBING THUMBNAILS THAT PERSUADE PEOPLE TO CLICK AND VIEW YOUR CONTENT.

BUILDING A NARRATIVE ARC WITHIN YOUR VIDEOS

A COMPELLING NARRATIVE ARC IS GENERALLY FOLLOWED BY EXCELLENT VIDEOS, WHICH HOLD VIEWERS' ATTENTION THROUGHOUT. RECOGNIZE THE COMPONENTS OF A STORY, FROM SETTING UP THE SCENE AND ADDING CONFLICT TO PROVIDING A SATISFYING CONCLUSION. DISCOVER HOW TO CREATE A GRIPPING STORY THAT KEEPS VIEWERS INTERESTED THROUGHOUT THE ENTIRE VIDEO.

OPTIMIZING VIDEO LENGTH AND PACING

To keep your viewers interested, find the ideal balance between the length and tempo of your videos. Examine methods for maximizing the duration of videos based on the kind of content and the expectations of viewers. Recognize how crucial timing is to preserving a lively and entertaining viewing experience.

ENHANCING VISUAL AND AUDIO QUALITY

In the realm of online video, quality counts. Discover how to improve the audio and visual quality of your material. This chapter gives you the tools to improve the production value of your videos, from selecting the appropriate gear and lighting to guaranteeing clear and crisp audio.

UTILIZING B-ROLL AND VISUAL ENHANCEMENTS

YOUR VIDEOS GET DEPTH AND VISUAL APPEAL FROM B-ROLL AND OTHER VISUAL UPGRADES. INVESTIGATE THE TECHNIQUE OF ADDING MORE VIDEO AND GRAPHICS TO YOUR CORE PIECE OF CONTENT. RECOGNIZE THE WAYS IN WHICH THESE IMPROVEMENTS IMPACT AUDIENCE HAPPINESS, ENGAGEMENT, AND STORYTELLING.

EFFECTIVE SCRIPTING AND ON-CAMERA PRESENCE

AN CRUCIAL SKILL FOR SCRIPTED CONTENT IS GOOD SCRIPTING. DEVELOP YOUR ABILITY TO WRITE COMPELLING, SUCCINCT, AND CLEAR SCRIPTS. EXAMINE METHODS FOR CONNECTING WITH YOUR AUDIENCE BY PRESENTING SCRIPTS ON CAMERA WITH CONFIDENCE AND HONESTY.

ENCOURAGING VIEWER INTERACTION AND PARTICIPATION

VIEWERS ARE KEPT INTERESTED AND A SENSE OF COMMUNITY IS PROMOTED BY INTERACTIVE COMPONENTS. EXAMINE METHODS FOR STIMULATING AUDIENCE PARTICIPATION, SUCH AS ASKING QUESTIONS, REQUESTING FEEDBACK, AND HOLDING SURVEYS AND COMPETITIONS. DISCOVER HOW TO TURN INACTIVE READERS INTO ENGAGED CONTRIBUTORS TO YOUR WORK.

UTILIZING END SCREENS AND CALLS TO ACTION (CTAS)

UTILIZE END SCREENS AND CALLS TO ACTION (CTAS) TO SUCCESSFULLY DIRECT YOUR VIEWERS ON THEIR NEXT STEPS. DISCOVER HOW TO MAKE EYE-CATCHING END SCREENS THAT ENTICE USERS TO SUBSCRIBE OR VIEW MORE MATERIAL. RECOGNIZE THE WAYS THAT WELL-PLACED CTAS CAN PROMOTE INTERACTION AND AID IN THE EXPANSION OF YOUR CHANNEL.

ANALYZING VIDEO PERFORMANCE AND VIEWER FEEDBACK

THE SECRET TO CONTENT STRATEGY IS CONSTANT IMPROVEMENT. EXPLORE THE PERFORMANCE OF VIDEOS USING ANALYTICS, LOOKING AT INDICATORS LIKE AS ENGAGEMENT, WATCH TIME, AND CLICK-THROUGH RATES. IN ORDER TO IMPROVE YOUR MATERIAL ACCORDING TO AUDIENCE PREFERENCES, YOU SHOULD ALSO LOOK INTO WAYS TO COLLECT AND ANALYZE VIEWER INPUT.

CONCLUSION CHAPTER 3 CRAFTING IMPACTFUL STORIES

AS WE GET TO THE END OF THIS CHAPTER, KEEP IN MIND THAT EVERY VIDEO PRESENTS AN OPPORTUNITY TO TELL A COMPELLING TALE. THE ART AND SCIENCE OF CONTENT DEVELOPMENT COMBINE TO PRODUCE VIDEOS THAT CONNECT, FROM KNOWING YOUR AUDIENCE TO OPTIMIZING TECHNICAL ELEMENTS. I HOPE THAT YOUR STORYTELLING PATH IS FULL OF ORIGINALITY, GENUINENESS, AND STRONG AUDIENCE CONNECTIONS. HAVE FUN WITH YOUR CREATIONS!

CHAPTER 4
MASTERING VIDEO
PRODUCTION TECHNIQUES

ELEVATING YOUR CRAFT

GREETINGS AND WELCOME TO "THE YOUTUBE LANDSCAPE UNVEILED," CHAPTER 4. THIS EPISODE DELVES DEEPLY INTO THE WORLD OF VIDEO CREATION AND REVEALS THE STRATEGIES THAT WILL HELP YOU CREATE MATERIAL THAT IS EVEN BETTER THAN BEFORE. YOUR ALL-INCLUSIVE GUIDE TO THE TECHNICAL FACETS OF PRODUCING VISUALLY SPECTACULAR AND EXPERTLY PRODUCED VIDEOS IS "MASTERING VIDEO PRODUCTION TECHNIQUES".

CHOOSING THE RIGHT EQUIPMENT

THE SELECTION OF APPROPRIATE EQUIPMENT IS THE CORNERSTONE OF A SUPERB VIDEO PRODUCTION. DISCOVER THE WORLD OF LIGHTING CONFIGURATIONS, MICROPHONES, LENSES, AND CAMERAS. THIS CHAPTER WALKS YOU THROUGH THE PROCESS OF CHOOSING EQUIPMENT THAT FITS BOTH YOUR CONTENT GOALS AND BUDGET, FROM ENTRY-LEVEL OPTIONS TO PROFESSIONAL GEAR.

UNDERSTANDING CAMERA SETTINGS AND MODES

Learn about the settings and modes of your camera to realize its full potential. To manage exposure, learn about principles like ISO, shutter speed, and aperture. Find out how using various shooting modes can improve your ability to be creative and produce visually striking videos.

OPTIMIZING LIGHTING FOR VIDEO

A key component of visual aesthetics is lighting. Examine methods for making the most of both artificial and natural lighting to improve your videos. This chapter gives you the tools to produce a well-lit and aesthetically pleasing scene, from three-point lighting setups to making the most of the light sources that are in your immediate environment.

CAPTURING HIGH-QUALITY AUDIO

IN VIDEO PRODUCTION, CLEAR AND SHARP AUDIO CANNOT BE COMPROMISED. EXPLORE THE WORLD OF AUDIO RECORDERS, MICROPHONES, AND METHODS FOR OBTAINING HIGH-QUALITY AUDIO RECORDINGS. DISCOVER HOW TO CAPTURE AUDIO FOR YOUR VIDEOS THAT SOUNDS GREAT, WHETHER IT'S VOICEOVERS, CONVERSATION, OR BACKGROUND NOISE.

MASTERING FRAMING AND COMPOSITION

THE CREATIVE COMPONENTS THAT LEND VISUAL APPEAL TO YOUR VIDEOS ARE COMPOSITION AND FRAMING. INVESTIGATE LEADING LINES, THE RULE OF THIRDS, AND OTHER COMPOSITIONAL STRATEGIES TO PRODUCE VISUALLY CAPTIVATING IMAGES. DISCOVER HOW TO PROPERLY FRAME SUBJECTS TO DIRECT THE VIEWER'S ATTENTION AND IMPROVE THE OVERALL LOOK.

EXPLORING DIFFERENT SHOOTING ANGLES

CHANGING UP YOUR SHOOTING ANGLES GIVES YOUR VIDEOS MORE ENERGY. THIS CHAPTER EXAMINES THE EFFECTS OF VARIOUS CAMERA ANGLES ON AUDIENCE INVOLVEMENT, RANGING FROM HIGH AND LOW ANGLES TO IMAGINATIVE VIEWPOINTS. RECOGNIZE WHICH ANGLES WILL BEST FIT YOUR MATERIAL AND BEST COMMUNICATE THE INFORMATION OR FEELINGS YOU WANT TO GET ACROSS.

UTILIZING MOVEMENT AND CAMERA TECHNIQUES

YOUR VIDEOS GAIN A DYNAMIC ELEMENT WHEN THERE IS MOVEMENT. INVESTIGATE CAMERA MOTIONS TO PRODUCE CINEMATIC SCENES, SUCH AS PANS, TILTS, AND TRACKING VIEWS. DISCOVER HOW TO EMPLOY MOVEMENT IN YOUR VIDEO PRODUCTION TO IMPROVE STORYTELLING, KEEP VIEWERS INTERESTED, AND PROJECT PROFESSIONALISM.

GREEN SCREEN AND VISUAL EFFECTS MASTERY

GREEN SCREENS PROVIDE COUNTLESS CREATIVE OPPORTUNITIES. LEARN HOW TO USE A GREEN SCREEN EFFECTIVELY AND INVESTIGATE SIMPLE VISUAL EFFECTS THAT MIGHT IMPROVE YOUR VIDEOS. THIS CHAPTER GIVES YOU AN INTRODUCTION TO THE WORLD OF POST-PRODUCTION MAGIC, COVERING EVERYTHING FROM MAKING VIRTUAL BACKGROUNDS TO ADDING STRAIGHTFORWARD CGI FEATURES.

EFFECTIVE VIDEO EDITING STRATEGIES

THE FINAL STEP IN PRODUCING A VIDEO IS EDITING IT TOGETHER. EXPLORE EFFICIENT TECHNIQUES FOR EDITING VIDEOS, SUCH AS USING TRANSITIONS, EFFECTS, AND COLOR GRADING, AS WELL AS ORGANIZING YOUR FOOTAGE AND CRAFTING A GRIPPING STORY. TO IMPROVE YOUR FILMS AND DELIVER THE MESSAGE YOU WANT, LEARN HOW TO USE EDITING SOFTWARE.

ADDING MUSIC AND SOUND EFFECTS

YOUR VIDEOS' EMOTIONAL IMPACT IS ENHANCED BY THE USE OF MUSIC AND SOUND EFFECTS. RECOGNIZE WHEN AND HOW TO INCLUDE MUSIC THAT IMPROVES YOUR MATERIAL. INVESTIGATE THE REALM OF SOUND EFFECTS TO ENHANCE REALISM AND DEPTH. DISCOVER HOW TO BALANCE AUDIO COMPONENTS FOR A PLEASING VIEWING EXPERIENCE.

OPTIMIZING VIDEO EXPORT SETTINGS

OPTIMIZING EXPORT SETTINGS FOR DISTRIBUTION IS THE LAST STAGE OF THE VIDEO CREATION PROCESS. EXAMINE THE OPTIMAL EXPORT CONFIGURATIONS FOR VARIOUS RESOLUTIONS AND PLATFORMS. DISCOVER HOW TO STRIKE A BALANCE BETWEEN FILE SIZE AND QUALITY TO MAKE SURE YOUR MOVIES APPEAR GREAT ON A VARIETY OF SCREENS AND INTERNET CONNECTIONS.

COLLABORATING WITH OTHER CREATORS AND PROFESSIONALS

WORKING TOGETHER BROADENS THE CREATIVE SCOPE. LEARN THE ADVANTAGES AND TACTICS OF WORKING WITH OTHER EXPERTS AND CREATORS. SEE HOW TEAMWORK MAY IMPROVE THE PRODUCTION QUALITY AND AUDIENCE FOR YOUR VIDEOS, WHETHER IT'S THROUGH COLLABORATIVE INITIATIVES, INVITED GUESTS, OR EMPLOYING EXPERTS.

CONTINUAL LEARNING AND SKILL DEVELOPMENT

THE ART OF PRODUCING VIDEOS IS ALWAYS CHANGING. ADOPT A MINDSET THAT EMPHASIZES LIFELONG LEARNING AND SKILL IMPROVEMENT. KEEP ABREAST WITH MARKET DEVELOPMENTS, EXPERIMENT WITH NOVEL APPROACHES, AND LOOK TO OTHER ARTISTS FOR INSPIRATION. YOU ARE ENCOURAGED IN THIS CHAPTER TO SEE EACH ENDEAVOR AS A CHANCE TO IMPROVE YOUR ABILITIES AND ELEVATE YOUR ART.

CONCLUSION CHAPTER 4
YOUR JOURNEY TO
VISUAL EXCELLENCE

REMEMBER THAT BECOMING AN EXPERT IN VIDEO CREATION IS A PROCESS RATHER THAN A FINAL GOAL AS WE WRAP UP THIS CHAPTER. EQUIPPED WITH TECHNICAL EXPERTISE AND A LOVE OF NARRATIVE, YOU MAY PRODUCE VIDEOS THAT ENTHRALL AND MOTIVATE VIEWERS IN ADDITION TO SHOWCASING YOUR MATERIAL. HAVE FUN WITH THE VIDEO!

CHAPTER 5
GROWING YOUR
SUBSCRIBER BASE

NURTURING YOUR
YOUTUBE COMMUNITY

GREETINGS AND WELCOME TO "THE YOUTUBE LANDSCAPE UNVEILED," CHAPTER 5. THIS EPISODE, WE DISCUSS THE KEY TO CREATING A COMMITTED COMMUNITY, WHICH IS INCREASING YOUR SUBSCRIBER BASE. "GROWING YOUR SUBSCRIBER BASE" DELVES INTO METHODS AND APPROACHES FOR DRAWING IN, INTERACTING WITH, AND KEEPING SUBSCRIBERS— ESSENTIALLY, CREATING A LIVELY AND ENCOURAGING COMMUNITY FOR YOUR CHANNEL.

UNDERSTANDING THE
IMPORTANCE OF
SUBSCRIBERS

THE CORE AUDIENCE OF YOUR CHANNEL CONSISTS OF ITS SUBSCRIBERS. EXAMINE THE ROLE THAT SUBSCRIBERS HAVE IN THE ANALYTICS, ALGORITHM, AND COMMUNITY INTERACTION OF YOUTUBE. RECOGNIZE THE BENEFITS OF HAVING A LARGE SUBSCRIBER BASE FOR YOUR CHANNEL'S PERFORMANCE AND VISIBILITY.

CREATING COMPELLING AND CONSISTENT CONTENT

THE FOUNDATION OF GROWING A SUBSCRIPTION BASE IS CONTENT. BECOME AN EXPERT AT PRODUCING CONTENT THAT APPEALS TO AND IS CONSISTENT WITH YOUR TARGET AUDIENCE. FIND OUT HOW A CLEAR CONTENT PLAN HELPS WITH BOTH ATTRACTING AND KEEPING SUBSCRIBERS.

ENGAGING VIEWERS THROUGH CALLS TO ACTION (CTAS)

CALLS TO ACTION (CTAS) THAT ARE WELL-PLANNED DIRECT VISITORS TO SUBSCRIBE TO AND INTERACT WITH YOUR CHANNEL. EXAMINE HOW TO INCLUDE CTAS IN YOUR DESCRIPTIONS, CHANNEL BANNERS, AND VIDEOS. FIND OUT HOW TO PERSUADE VISITORS TO TAKE AN ACTIVE ROLE IN YOUR EXPANDING COMMUNITY.

UTILIZING PLAYLISTS FOR VIEWER RETENTION

PLAYLISTS ARE AN EFFECTIVE WAY TO KEEP VIEWERS INTERESTED AND MOTIVATE THEM TO STAY ON THE SHOW LONGER. EXAMINE PLAYLIST CREATION AND ORGANIZATION TECHNIQUES THAT IMPROVE VIEWER RETENTION. FIND OUT HOW PLAYLISTS IMPROVE THE VIEWING EXPERIENCE OVERALL AND BOOST THE POSSIBILITY THAT VIEWERS WILL BECOME SUBSCRIBERS.

PROMOTING YOUR CHANNEL ON SOCIAL MEDIA

SOCIAL MEDIA EXPANDS THE AUDIENCE FOR YOUR CHANNEL. LEARN THE TECHNIQUE OF USING DIFFERENT SOCIAL MEDIA CHANNELS TO PROMOTE YOUR CHANNEL AND CONTENT. EXAMINE SUCCESSFUL METHODS FOR INTERACTING WITH CURRENT SUBSCRIBERS AND DRAWING IN NEW ONES ON SOCIAL MEDIA SITES LIKE FACEBOOK, INSTAGRAM, AND TWITTER.

COLLABORATING WITH OTHER YOUTUBERS

PARTNERSHIPS BRING YOUR CHANNEL IN FRONT OF NEW VIEWERS. EXPLORE THE REALM OF WORKING TOGETHER WITH OTHER YOUTUBERS. DISCOVER HOW TO FIND POSSIBLE PARTNERS, PRESENT IDEAS FOR PARTNERSHIPS, AND PRODUCE CONTENT THAT BENEFITS BOTH PLATFORMS. PARTNERSHIPS HAVE THE POTENTIAL TO BE A POTENT GROWTH ENGINE FOR SUBSCRIBERS.

RUNNING CONTESTS AND GIVEAWAYS

GIVEAWAYS AND CONTESTS INFUSE YOUR CHANNEL WITH EXCITEMENT. EXAMINE HOW CONTESTS CAN BE USED STRATEGICALLY TO PROMOTE PARTICIPATION, SHARING, AND SUBSCRIPTIONS. DEVELOP A SENSE OF CAMARADERIE AND EXCITEMENT AMONG YOUR VIEWERS BY LEARNING HOW TO MANAGE CONTESTS SUCCESSFULLY AND IN COMPLIANCE WITH YOUTUBE'S RESTRICTIONS.

OPTIMIZING CHANNEL SEO FOR DISCOVERY

ONE OF THE MOST IMPORTANT ASPECTS OF CHANNEL DISCOVERY IS SEARCH ENGINE OPTIMIZATION, OR SEO. EXAMINE METHODS FOR IMPROVING THE SEARCH ENGINE OPTIMIZATION OF YOUR CHANNEL AND INDIVIDUAL VIDEOS. DISCOVER HOW TO MAKE THE MOST OUT OF TITLES, DESCRIPTIONS, TAGS, AND KEYWORDS TO DRAW IN MORE SUBSCRIBERS AND MAKE YOUR MATERIAL MORE VISIBLE.

ENGAGING WITH YOUR AUDIENCE THROUGH COMMENTS

CREATING A SENSE OF COMMUNITY WITH YOUR AUDIENCE REQUIRES ACTIVE INTERACTION. EXAMINE METHODS FOR LEAVING COMMENTS, POSING QUERIES, AND PROMOTING DIALOGUE. DISCOVER THE WAYS THAT SINCERE COMMUNICATION NOT ONLY IMPROVES YOUR RELATIONSHIP WITH CURRENT SUBSCRIBERS BUT ALSO ENTICES NEW ONES TO SIGN UP.

HOSTING LIVE STREAMS AND PREMIERE EVENTS

OPPORTUNITIES FOR IN-THE-MOMENT PARTICIPATION ARE PROVIDED BY LIVE STREAMING AND PREMIER EVENTS. EXAMINE THE ADVANTAGES OF PRESENTING MOVIES AND HOLDING LIVE SESSIONS. FIND OUT HOW THESE OCCASIONS ENGENDER A FEELING OF URGENCY AND EXCLUSIVITY THAT ENTICES VIEWERS TO SUBSCRIBE AND ENGAGE WITH YOUR CHANNEL'S COMMUNITY.

ANALYZING ANALYTICS FOR SUBSCRIBER INSIGHTS

ANALYTICS GIVE YOU IMPORTANT INFORMATION ABOUT THE BEHAVIOR OF YOUR AUDIENCE. EXPLORE YOUTUBE ANALYTICS TO LEARN ABOUT THE DEMOGRAPHICS, VIEW DURATION, AND ENGAGEMENT OF YOUR SUBSCRIBERS. ACQUIRE THE KNOWLEDGE OF DATA INTERPRETATION TO IMPROVE YOUR CONTENT STRATEGY AND CUSTOMIZE YOUR APPROACH TO SUCCESSFULLY DRAW IN AND HOLD ONTO SUBSCRIBERS.

OFFERING EXCLUSIVE CONTENT FOR SUBSCRIBERS

YOUR SUBSCRIBERS GAIN VALUE FROM EXCLUSIVE MATERIAL. EXAMINE METHODS FOR PROVIDING YOUR SUBSCRIBERS WITH BONUSES, BEHIND-THE-SCENES MATERIAL, OR SPECIAL VIDEOS. FIND OUT HOW TO CREATE A FEELING OF EXCLUSIVITY TO ENTICE VISITORS TO SUBSCRIBE AND TURN INTO DEVOTED MEMBERS OF YOUR GROUP.

IMPLEMENTING CHANNEL BRANDING FOR RECOGNITION

MAINTAINING A CONSISTENT BRAND IMPROVES TRUST AND RECOGNITION. EXAMINE THE SIGNIFICANCE OF INTROS, BANNERS, AND LOGOS FOR CHANNEL BRANDING. DISCOVER HOW A UNIFIED BRAND IMAGE HELPS CREATE A POLISHED, MEMORABLE CHANNEL THAT ENTICES USERS TO SUBSCRIBE FOR MORE CONTENT.

CROSS-PROMOTING YOUR VIDEOS

CROSS-PROMOTION INCREASES YOUR CONTENT'S VISIBILITY TO ITS FULLEST. EXAMINE METHODS FOR GETTING VISITORS TO WATCH RELATED VIDEOS ON YOUR CHANNEL BY PROMOTING YOUR VIDEOS WITHIN YOUR OWN CONTENT. FIND OUT HOW TO USE CLEVER CROSS-PROMOTION TO MAKE VIEWERS MORE LIKELY TO SUBSCRIBE WHEN THEY COME ACROSS MORE OF YOUR MATERIAL.

CREATING COMPELLING CHANNEL TRAILERS FOR NEW VIEWERS

FOR NEW VIEWERS, YOUR CHANNEL TEASER SETS THE TONE EARLY. LEARN HOW TO DESIGN A CAPTIVATING CHANNEL TRAILER THAT CLEARLY CONVEYS THE VALUE PROPOSITION OF YOUR CHANNEL. FIND OUT HOW TO CREATE A CAPTIVATING TEASER THAT ENTICES VISITORS TO SUBSCRIBE AND CHECK OUT MORE OF YOUR STUFF.

CONCLUSION CHAPTER 5 NURTURING YOUR GROWING COMMUNITY

As we come to the end of this chapter, keep in mind that developing community and cultivating relationships are key components of building your subscriber base. In addition to drawing in new members, the tactics discussed in this chapter are designed to build a community of interested and supportive readers. May the good times and prosperity of your community never end. Happy expanding!

CHAPTER 6
MONETIZATION STRATEGIES FOR CREATORS

TURNING PASSION INTO PROFIT

GREETINGS AND WELCOME TO "THE YOUTUBE LANDSCAPE UNVEILED," CHAPTER 6. THIS CHAPTER DELVES INTO THE FASCINATING WORLD OF LEVERAGING SUCCESSFUL MONETIZATION TACTICS TO TRANSFORM YOUR PASSION INTO PROFIT. "MONETIZATION STRATEGIES FOR CREATORS" GIVES YOU TIPS ON HOW TO MAKE MONEY FROM YOUR YOUTUBE CHANNEL WITHOUT SACRIFICING THE QUALITY OF EXPERIENCE FOR YOUR VIEWERS.

UNDERSTANDING YOUTUBE'S MONETIZATION PROGRAMS

THROUGH A NUMBER OF INITIATIVES, YOUTUBE GIVES CONTENT CREATORS THE CHANCE TO MAKE MONEY OFF OF THEIR WORK. EXAMINE THE SPECIFICS OF INITIATIVES LIKE ADSENSE, CHANNEL MEMBERSHIPS, YOUTUBE PARTNER PROGRAM (YPP), AND RETAIL SHELVES. RECOGNIZE THE PREREQUISITES AND ELIGIBILITY REQUIREMENTS IN ORDER TO PARTICIPATE IN THESE PROGRAMS.

SETTING UP AND OPTIMIZING ADSENSE FOR REVENUE

When it comes to making money from your films, AdSense is a major factor. Examine how to set up and optimize AdSense to get the most out of your revenue. To increase your overall revenue, learn about ad types, ad placements, and CPM (Cost Per Mille) tactics.

MAXIMIZING REVENUE WITH AD PLACEMENT STRATEGIES

Your earnings might be considerably impacted by well-placed advertisements. Explore methods for thoughtfully inserting advertisements into your films. Find out more about sponsored cards, overlay advertisements, and mid-roll ads. Recognize how to strike a balance between ad placement and viewer experience to maximize revenue.

LEVERAGING CHANNEL MEMBERSHIPS FOR EXCLUSIVE CONTENT

WITH CHANNEL MEMBERSHIPS, FANS MAY DIRECTLY CONTRIBUTE TO THE FINANCIAL SUPPORT OF CREATORS. EXAMINE THE ADVANTAGES OF ESTABLISHING CHANNEL MEMBERSHIPS, SUCH AS PROVIDING PAYING USERS WITH UNIQUE EMOJIS, BADGES, AND SPECIAL BONUSES. DISCOVER HOW TO ORGANIZE YOUR MEMBERSHIP LEVELS AND PRODUCE ENGAGING CONTENT FOR YOUR DEVOTED FOLLOWERS.

UTILIZING THE MERCHANDISE SHELF FOR PRODUCT SALES

THE MERCHANDISE SHELF SERVES AS YOUR CHANNEL'S PHYSICAL STOREFRONT WHERE YOU CAN SELL GOODS. EXPLORE THE METHOD OF ASSEMBLING AND EMPLOYING THE MERCHANDISE SHELF TO MARKET AND SELL ITEMS BEARING YOUR BRAND. EXAMINE METHODS FOR PRODUCING ENTICING PRODUCTS AND INCREASING CHANNEL SALES.

EXPLORING AFFILIATE MARKETING OPPORTUNITIES

AFFILIATE MARKETING GIVES AUTHORS ACCESS TO A SECOND SOURCE OF INCOME. BY COLLABORATING WITH COMPANIES AND ADVERTISING THEIR GOODS OR SERVICES, YOU CAN LEARN MORE ABOUT THE REALM OF AFFILIATE MARKETING. DISCOVER HOW TO THOUGHTFULLY ADD AFFILIATE LINKS TO YOUR CONTENT WITHOUT COMPROMISING YOUR AUDIENCE'S TRUST OR SENSE OF AUTHENTICITY.

NEGOTIATING SPONSORED CONTENT DEALS

CREATORS CAN WORK WITH BRANDS ON SPONSORED CONTENT IN EXCHANGE FOR FINANCIAL REMUNERATION. EXPLORE THE ART OF ARRANGING DEALS FOR SPONSORED CONTENT. DISCOVER HOW TO FIND THE RIGHT PARTNERSHIPS, CRAFT PERSUASIVE PROPOSALS, AND MAKE SURE SPONSORED CONTENT FITS THE INTERESTS AND VALUES OF YOUR CHANNEL.

PARTICIPATING IN YOUTUBE'S SUPER CHAT AND SUPER STICKERS

DURING LIVE STREAMING, FANS CAN DIRECTLY SUPPORT CREATORS VIA SUPER CHAT AND SUPER STICKERS. EXAMINE THESE INTERACTIVE MONETIZATION TECHNOLOGIES' FEATURES AND ADVANTAGES. DISCOVER HOW TO CREATE CAPTIVATING LIVE STREAMS THAT DRAW CONTRIBUTIONS FROM SUPER CHAT AND INSPIRE VIEWER INTERACTION.

DIVERSIFYING INCOME STREAMS WITH PATREON INTEGRATION

THROUGH PATREON, CREATORS MAY ACCESS A PLATFORM WHERE THEIR AUDIENCE CAN GRANT THEM CONTINUOUS SUPPORT. EXPLORE THE PROCESS OF LINKING YOUR YOUTUBE CHANNEL TO PATREON. INVESTIGATE HOW TO INCREASE THE VARIETY OF YOUR REVENUE STREAMS BY PROVIDING YOUR PATREON BACKERS WITH SPECIAL MATERIAL, BENEFITS, AND INCENTIVES.

UNDERSTANDING THE IMPORTANCE OF VIEWER LOYALTY

STRATEGY FOR MONETIZATION THRIVES ON AUDIENCE LOYALTY. EXAMINE THE SIGNIFICANCE OF ATTRACTING AND RETAINING A DEVOTED FOLLOWING. FIND OUT HOW TO BUILD A SENSE OF COMMUNITY, INTERACT WITH YOUR AUDIENCE, AND CONTINUALLY PRODUCE HIGH-QUALITY CONTENT TO INCREASE VIEWER LOYALTY AND LONG-TERM FINANCIAL VIABILITY.

NAVIGATING THE CHALLENGES OF DEMONETIZATION

ONE ISSUE THAT MANY CREATORS MAY ENCOUNTER IS DEMONETIZATION. RECOGNIZE THE CAUSES OF DEMONETIZATION AND INVESTIGATE WAYS TO PREVENT OR ADDRESS IT. FIND OUT HOW TO MODIFY YOUR CONTENT STRATEGY SO THAT IT COMPLIES WITH YOUTUBE'S RULES AND STILL MAKES MONEY.

STAYING INFORMED ON YOUTUBE'S MONETIZATION POLICIES

THE RULES AND REGULATIONS ON YOUTUBE CHANGE WITH TIME. KEEP UP WITH THE MOST RECENT ADJUSTMENTS AND MODIFICATIONS TO YOUTUBE'S MONETIZATION GUIDELINES. EXAMINE AVAILABLE CHANNELS AND TOOLS TO STAY INFORMED ABOUT POLICY CHANGES AND TO MAKE SURE YOU'RE ADHERING TO THE PLATFORM'S RULES.

OPTIMIZING THUMBNAIL AND TITLE STRATEGIES FOR CLICK-THROUGHS

A HIGHER CLICK-THROUGH RATE RAISES AUDIENCE ENGAGEMENT AND AD REVENUE. EXAMINE METHODS FOR IMPROVING TITLES AND THUMBNAILS TO PROMOTE INCREASED CLICK-THROUGH RATES. TO IMPROVE YOUR STRATEGY AND INCREASE EARNING POSSIBILITIES, LEARN ABOUT ATTENTION-GRABBING GRAPHICS, CONCISE TITLES, AND A/B TESTING.

CONCLUSION CHAPTER 6 MONETIZING WITH INTEGRITY AND PURPOSE

AS WE GET TO THE END OF THIS CHAPTER, KEEP IN MIND THAT SUCCESSFUL MONETIZATION INVOLVES MORE THAN JUST TURNING A PROFIT—IT ALSO INVOLVES MAINTAINING YOUR CREATIVE ENTHUSIASM AND OFFERING VALUE TO YOUR AUDIENCE. THROUGH THE ETHICAL AND PURPOSEFUL INTEGRATION OF VARIOUS MONETIZATION TACTICS, YOU MAY TRANSFORM YOUR YOUTUBE CHANNEL INTO A PROFITABLE ENTERPRISE. CHEERS TO YOUR PROFITABLE VENTURE!

CHAPTER 7
SOCIAL MEDIA INTEGRATION
FOR AMPLIFIED REACH

EXPANDING YOUR INFLUENCE
BEYOND YOUTUBE

GREETINGS AND WELCOME TO "THE YOUTUBE LANDSCAPE UNVEILED," CHAPTER 7. WE DISCUSS HOW TO USE SOCIAL MEDIA INTEGRATION TO REACH A WIDER AUDIENCE AND INCREASE THE EFFECTIVENESS OF YOUR CONTENT IN THIS SECTION. THE BOOK "SOCIAL MEDIA INTEGRATION FOR AMPLIFIED REACH" OFFERS ADVICE ON HOW TO STRATEGICALLY USE DIFFERENT SOCIAL MEDIA CHANNELS.

UNDERSTANDING THE ROLE OF
SOCIAL MEDIA IN CONTENT
PROMOTION

SOCIAL MEDIA PLATFORMS ARE EFFECTIVE INSTRUMENTS FOR PROMOTING CONTENT AND FOSTERING AUDIENCE INTERACTION. EXPLORE HOW SOCIAL MEDIA MAY HELP YOU REACH A WIDER AUDIENCE WITH YOUR CONTENT, ATTRACT MORE VIEWERS TO YOUR YOUTUBE CHANNEL, AND BUILD A COMMUNITY THAT EXTENDS BEYOND THE PLATFORM.

CHOOSING THE RIGHT SOCIAL MEDIA PLATFORMS

SOCIAL MEDIA NETWORKS ARE NOT MADE EQUALLY. EXAMINE THE FEATURES OF POPULAR PLATFORMS LIKE FACEBOOK, INSTAGRAM, TWITTER, AND OTHERS. DISCOVER HOW TO SELECT THE PLATFORMS THAT WILL BEST SERVE YOUR INTENDED AUDIENCE, TYPE OF CONTENT, AND PROMOTION OBJECTIVES.

OPTIMIZING YOUR SOCIAL MEDIA PROFILES

YOUR SOCIAL MEDIA ACCOUNTS SERVE AS BRAND EXTENSIONS. TAKE A DEEP DIVE INTO IMPROVING YOUR PROFILES ACROSS SEVERAL PLATFORMS. DISCOVER HOW TO WRITE CAPTIVATING BIOS, SELECT EYE-CATCHING PROFILE PHOTOS, AND PROVIDE CONNECTIONS TO OTHER PERTINENT CONTENT AND YOUR YOUTUBE CHANNEL.

CREATING SHAREABLE SNIPPETS AND TEASERS

Teases and morsels that are easy to post can entice your social media following. Examine methods for producing interesting and viral material that offers a sneak peek at your YouTube videos. Discover how to use these snippets to promote your channel and increase visitors.

ESTABLISHING A POSTING SCHEDULE FOR CONSISTENCY

Engaging on social media requires consistency. Examine the significance of creating a publishing schedule that corresponds with your calendar of content. Find out how regular posting encourages interaction from your audience, creates suspense, and helps your followers remember your content.

LEVERAGING HASHTAGS FOR DISCOVERABILITY

UTILIZING HASHTAGS EFFECTIVELY CAN BOOST A POST'S DISCOVERABILITY ON SOCIAL MEDIA SITES LIKE TWITTER AND INSTAGRAM. DISCOVER HOW TO USE HASHTAGS STRATEGICALLY. DISCOVER HOW TO FIND AND SELECT PERTINENT HASHTAGS THAT COMPLEMENT YOUR CONTENT TO GROW YOUR BLOG'S EXPOSURE AND GAIN MORE FOLLOWERS.

ENGAGING WITH YOUR SOCIAL MEDIA COMMUNITY

IT'S IMPERATIVE THAT YOU PARTICIPATE ACTIVELY IN YOUR SOCIAL MEDIA NETWORK. EXAMINE VARIOUS APPROACHES FOR ANSWERING MENTIONS, DIRECT MESSAGES, AND COMMENTS. DEVELOP RELATIONSHIPS WITH YOUR FOLLOWERS, START CONVERSATIONS WITH THEM, AND MOTIVATE THEM TO TELL THEIR NETWORKS ABOUT YOUR MATERIAL.

CROSS-PROMOTING BETWEEN PLATFORMS

CROSS-PROMOTION EXPANDS THE AUDIENCE FOR YOUR MATERIAL. LEARN HOW TO CROSS-PROMOTE YOUR YOUTUBE VIDEOS ON VARIOUS SOCIAL MEDIA NETWORKS. DISCOVER HOW TO CUSTOMIZE YOUR STRATEGY FOR EVERY PLATFORM, MODIFYING YOUR MATERIAL TO FIT THE CHARACTERISTICS AND TASTES OF YOUR SOCIAL MEDIA FOLLOWING.

HOSTING LIVE Q&A SESSIONS AND AMAS

INTERACTIVE ENGAGEMENT OPTIONS ARE OFFERED BY ASK ME ANYTHING (AMA) EVENTS AND LIVE Q&A SESSIONS. EXPLORE THE ART OF CONDUCTING LIVE EVENTS ON SOCIAL MEDIA SITES SUCH AS TWITTER OR INSTAGRAM. DEVELOP YOUR ABILITY TO INVITE QUESTIONS, ENGAGE YOUR AUDIENCE IN REAL TIME, AND FOSTER A FEELING OF COMMUNITY.

UTILIZING INSTAGRAM STORIES AND REELS FOR VISUAL IMPACT

INSTAGRAM OFFERS OPTIONS FOR DYNAMIC VISUAL STORYTELLING THROUGH FEATURES LIKE REELS AND STORIES. EXAMINE TECHNIQUES FOR UTILIZING THESE TOOLS TO PRODUCE VISUALLY STRIKING CONTENT THAT ENHANCES YOUR YOUTUBE CHANNEL. DISCOVER THE BEST WAYS TO REPURPOSE CONTENT TO GET THE MOST INTERACTION POSSIBLE.

RUNNING CONTESTS AND GIVEAWAYS ON SOCIAL MEDIA

SOCIAL MEDIA SITES THAT HOST FREEBIES AND CONTESTS ENCOURAGE PARTICIPATION AND EXCITEMENT. TAKE A DEEP DIVE INTO ORGANIZING AND CARRYING OUT GIVEAWAYS AND CONTESTS. DISCOVER HOW TO TAKE ADVANTAGE OF THESE OCCASIONS TO PROMOTE ENGAGEMENT, GROW YOUR SOCIAL MEDIA FAN BASE, AND ENHANCE TRAFFIC TO YOUR YOUTUBE CHANNEL.

COLLABORATING WITH INFLUENCERS AND PEERS

WORKING TOGETHER WITH PEERS AND INFLUENCERS GREATLY INCREASES YOUR REACH. EXPLORE THE SKILL OF WORKING WITH PEOPLE WHO COMMAND A SIZABLE SOCIAL MEDIA FOLLOWING. DISCOVER HOW TO FIND POSSIBLE PARTNERS, PRESENT IDEAS FOR PARTNERSHIPS, AND PRODUCE MATERIAL THAT SERVES BOTH SIDES EQUALLY.

ANALYZING SOCIAL MEDIA ANALYTICS FOR STRATEGY REFINEMENT

SOCIAL MEDIA ANALYTICS OFFER INSIGHTFUL INFORMATION ON THE ACTIONS OF YOUR AUDIENCE. EXPLORE THE ANALYTICS TOOLS OFFERED BY SOCIAL MEDIA SITES LIKE FACEBOOK, INSTAGRAM, AND TWITTER. ACQUIRE THE KNOWLEDGE OF DATA INTERPRETATION TO ENHANCE YOUR SOCIAL MEDIA TACTICS, SPOT PATTERNS, AND MAXIMIZE THE EFFECTIVENESS OF YOUR APPROACH.

OPTIMIZING LINKEDIN FOR PROFESSIONAL NETWORKING

LINKEDIN PROVIDES EXCEPTIONAL CHANCES FOR CONTENT PROMOTION AND BUSINESS NETWORKING. EXAMINE METHODS FOR ENHANCING YOUR LINKEDIN PROFILE, EXCHANGING INDUSTRY INSIGHTS, AND ESTABLISHING CONNECTIONS WITH EXPERTS IN YOUR FIELD. DISCOVER HOW TO LEVERAGE LINKEDIN TO INCREASE YOUR INDUSTRY REACH AND CREDIBILITY.

CONCLUSION CHAPTER 7 BUILDING A MULTI-PLATFORM PRESENCE

AS WE COME TO THE END OF THIS CHAPTER, KEEP IN MIND THAT HAVING A MULTI-PLATFORM PRESENCE INCREASES THE IMPACT OF YOUR CONTENT AND INCREASES YOUR TOTAL INFLUENCE. THROUGH DELIBERATE INCORPORATION OF SOCIAL MEDIA INTO YOUR CONTENT MARKETING PLAN, YOU MAY ESTABLISH A UNIFIED AND COMPREHENSIVE ONLINE PRESENCE. CHEERS TO YOUR SOCIALIZING!

CHAPTER 8
BUILDING BRAND PARTNERSHIPS AND COLLABORATIONS

ELEVATING YOUR CHANNEL THROUGH STRATEGIC ALLIANCES

GREETINGS AND WELCOME TO "THE YOUTUBE LANDSCAPE UNVEILED," CHAPTER 8. TO IMPROVE YOUR CHANNEL AND FORGE WIN-WIN CONNECTIONS, WE DELVE INTO THE ART OF FORMING BRAND ALLIANCES AND PARTNERSHIPS IN THIS SECTION. THE BOOK "BUILDING BRAND PARTNERSHIPS AND COLLABORATIONS" OFFERS GUIDANCE ON HOW TO DEVELOP BUSINESS PARTNERSHIPS AND COOPERATIVE RELATIONSHIPS WITH BRANDS AND OTHER ARTISTS.

UNDERSTANDING THE VALUE OF BRAND PARTNERSHIPS

CREATORS CAN BENEFIT FROM A VARIETY OF CONTENT OPPORTUNITIES, MORE VISIBILITY, AND FINANCIAL SUPPORT THROUGH BRAND RELATIONSHIPS. EXAMINE THE BENEFITS OF BRAND COLLABORATIONS AND HOW THEY CAN SUPPORT THE EXPANSION AND LONG-TERM VIABILITY OF YOUR CHANNEL.

DEFINING YOUR BRAND AND UNIQUE SELLING PROPOSITION (USP)

ESTABLISH YOUR BRAND IDENTITY AND UNIQUE SELLING PROPOSITION (USP) PRIOR TO PURSUING PARTNERSHIPS. EXAMINE METHODS FOR COMMUNICATING YOUR TARGET MARKET, YOUR BRAND'S VALUES, AND THE UNIQUE FEATURES THAT MAKE YOUR CHANNEL STAND OUT. HAVING A DISTINCT BRAND IDENTITY MAKES YOU MORE APPEALING TO POSSIBLE PARTNERS.

IDENTIFYING AND RESEARCHING POTENTIAL BRAND PARTNERS

FINDING AND INVESTIGATING POSSIBLE BRAND PARTNERS IS THE FIRST STEP IN CREATING A STRATEGIC COLLABORATION. TAKE A DEEP DIVE INTO ASSESSING COMPANIES THAT FIT YOUR AUDIENCE, VALUES, AND CONTENT. TO MAKE WISE SELECTIONS ABOUT PARTNERSHIPS, LEARN HOW TO EVALUATE A BRAND'S REPUTATION, TARGET MARKET, AND PAST PARTNERSHIPS.

CRAFTING AN EFFECTIVE PARTNERSHIP PROPOSAL

DEVELOPING A STRONG PARTNERSHIP PROPOSAL IS ESSENTIAL TO DRAWING IN BRANDS. EXAMINE THE KEY COMPONENTS OF A PARTNERSHIP PROPOSAL, SUCH AS A SYNOPSIS OF YOUR CHANNEL, INSIGHTS INTO YOUR TARGET AUDIENCE, AND THE UNIQUE BENEFITS YOU CAN PROVIDE TO THE COMPANY. DISCOVER HOW TO MODIFY PROPOSALS TO FIT THE OBJECTIVES AND REQUIREMENTS OF POSSIBLE PARTNERS.

NEGOTIATING TERMS AND DELIVERABLES

ONE OF THE MOST IMPORTANT STEPS IN CREATING EFFECTIVE COLLABORATIONS IS NEGOTIATION. EXPLORE THE ART OF NEGOTIATING DELIVERABLES AND AGREEMENTS WITH BRANDS. ACQUIRE THE SKILLS NECESSARY TO SPECIFY DUTIES, SET EXPECTATIONS, AND MAKE SURE THAT THE AGREEMENT BENEFITS BOTH SIDES EQUALLY.

MAINTAINING AUTHENTICITY IN BRAND COLLABORATIONS

RETAINING YOUR AUDIENCE'S TRUST REQUIRES BEING GENUINE. EXAMINE METHODS FOR INCORPORATING BRAND PARTNERSHIPS INTO YOUR WRITING WITHOUT SACRIFICING YOUR DISTINCT VOICE OR STYLE. DISCOVER HOW TO CREATE PROMOTIONAL CONTENT THAT IS BOTH HONEST AND APPEALING TO YOUR TARGET AUDIENCE.

LEVERAGING AFFILIATE MARKETING IN BRAND COLLABORATIONS

BRAND PARTNERSHIPS CAN BENEFIT GREATLY FROM THE USE OF AFFILIATE MARKETING. EXAMINE VARIOUS APPROACHES FOR ADDING AFFILIATE CODES AND CONNECTIONS TO SPONSORED CONTENT. FIND OUT HOW TO GIVE YOUR AUDIENCE VALUE WHILE MAXIMIZING MONEY VIA AFFILIATE AGREEMENTS.

CREATING ENGAGING SPONSORED CONTENT

CREATING INTERESTING SPONSORED CONTENT IS ESSENTIAL TO DRAWING IN VIEWERS. EXAMINE METHODS FOR PRODUCING SPONSORED VIDEOS THAT YOUR AUDIENCE FINDS ENGAGING. DISCOVER HOW TO EFFECTIVELY INCORPORATE BRAND MESSAGING, HIGHLIGHT GOODS OR SERVICES, AND KEEP VIEWERS INTERESTED THROUGHOUT SPONSORED CONTENT.

MEASURING THE SUCCESS OF BRAND COLLABORATIONS

COLLABORATIONS BETWEEN BRANDS ARE SUCCESSFUL WHEN THEY ARE MEASURED EFFECTIVELY. EXAMINE ANALYTICS TOOLS AND KEY PERFORMANCE INDICATORS (KPIS) TO DETERMINE THE EFFECT OF SPONSORED CONTENT. TO GIVE YOUR PARTNERS USEFUL INFORMATION, LEARN HOW TO TRACK ENGAGEMENT, CLICK-THROUGH RATES, AND OVERALL BRAND VISIBILITY.

BUILDING LONG-TERM RELATIONSHIPS WITH BRANDS

ESTABLISHING ENDURING CONNECTIONS WITH BRANDS IS A FACTOR IN LONG-TERM SUCCESS. EXAMINE METHODS FOR FOSTERING CONNECTIONS THAT GO BEYOND A SINGLE PROJECT. DISCOVER HOW TO CONSISTENTLY ADD VALUE FOR BUSINESSES, GO ABOVE AND BEYOND WHAT IS EXPECTED OF YOU, AND ESTABLISH YOURSELF AS A DEPENDABLE AND TRUSTWORTHY PARTNER FOR NEXT PROJECTS.

COLLABORATING WITH FELLOW CREATORS FOR CROSS-PROMOTION

COLLABORATING WITH OTHER ARTISTS PROVIDES SPECIAL CHANCES FOR CROSS-PROMOTION. EXPLORE THE ADVANTAGES OF WORKING WITH COLLEAGUES IN YOUR FIELD. FIND OUT HOW CROSS-PROMOTING IMPROVES YOUR CONTENT, GROWS YOUR AUDIENCE, AND FOSTERS A POSITIVE INDUSTRY COMMUNITY.

NAVIGATING CHALLENGES AND MITIGATING RISKS

RISK REDUCTION IS ESSENTIAL SINCE BRAND COLLABORATIONS MAY FACE DIFFICULTIES. EXAMINE TYPICAL PROBLEMS LIKE EXPECTATIONS OR VALUES THAT AREN'T ALIGNED. UNDERSTAND HOW TO DEAL WITH THESE ISSUES HEAD-ON AND PUT RISK-REDUCTION MEASURES IN PLACE TO MAKE SURE THAT COLLABORATIONS GO SMOOTHLY.

ENSURING LEGAL COMPLIANCE IN PARTNERSHIPS

ADHERENCE TO THE LAW IS CRUCIAL IN BRAND COLLABORATIONS. EXAMINE FACTORS INCLUDING CONTRACT CONDITIONS, INTELLECTUAL PROPERTY RIGHTS, AND TRANSPARENCY REQUIREMENTS. FIND OUT HOW TO MAKE SURE YOUR PARTNERSHIPS UPHOLD THE LAW AND SAFEGUARD EACH PARTY'S INTERESTS.

SHOWCASING SUCCESSFUL COLLABORATIONS ON YOUR CHANNEL

DISPLAYING SUCCESSFUL PARTNERSHIPS RAISES THE LEGITIMACY OF YOUR CHANNEL. INVESTIGATE METHODS FOR EMPHASIZING BRAND ALLIANCES ON YOUR CHANNEL. DISCOVER HOW TO PRODUCE SPECIFIC FEATURES OR CONTENT THAT HONORS PARTNERSHIPS AND GIVES YOUR PARTNERS MORE EXPOSURE.

CONCLUSION CHAPTER 8 CULTIVATING LASTING PARTNERSHIPS

AS WE GET TO THE END OF THIS CHAPTER, KEEP IN MIND THAT DEVELOPING ENDURING RELATIONSHIPS CALLS FOR A TRIFECTA OF PROFESSIONALISM, SINCERITY, AND STRATEGIC ALIGNMENT. YOU CAN IMPROVE YOUR CHANNEL, YOUR CONTENT, AND THE COLLABORATIVE COMMUNITY YOU BUILD WITH OTHER CREATORS BY BUILDING TIES WITH BUSINESSES AND OTHER CREATIVES. THIS WILL APPEAL TO YOUR AUDIENCE. CHEERS TO YOUR SUCCESSFUL PARTNERSHIP!

CHAPTER 9
ANALYTICS AND DATA-DRIVEN GROWTH

NAVIGATING THE DIGITAL LANDSCAPE WITH INSIGHT

GREETINGS AND WELCOME TO "THE YOUTUBE LANDSCAPE UNVEILED," CHAPTER 9. WE DISCUSS THE VALUE OF ANALYTICS AND DATA-DRIVEN INITIATIVES IN THIS SEGMENT TO HELP YOU BUILD YOUR CHANNEL. "ANALYTICS AND DATA-DRIVEN GROWTH" GIVES ADVICE ON HOW TO USE DATA TO IMPROVE THE EFFECTIVENESS OF YOUR CONTENT OVERALL AND MAKE WISE JUDGMENTS.

UNDERSTANDING THE POWER OF ANALYTICS

IN THE DIGITAL WORLD, ANALYTICS ACT AS A COMPASS, DIRECTING PRODUCERS TOWARD CALCULATED CHOICES. EXPLORE THE POTENTIAL OF ANALYTICS AND HOW INSIGHTS DERIVED FROM DATA MAY DRIVE THE EXPANSION OF YOUR CHANNEL. RECOGNIZE THE IMPORTANT PARAMETERS THAT AFFECT THE SUCCESS AND AUDIENCE ENGAGEMENT OF YOUR CHANNEL.

NAVIGATING YOUTUBE ANALYTICS: AN IN-DEPTH OVERVIEW

FOR CREATORS, YOUTUBE ANALYTICS IS A TREASURE TROVE OF DATA. EXAMINE A COMPREHENSIVE SUMMARY OF YOUTUBE ANALYTICS, ENCOMPASSING IMPORTANT SEGMENTS LIKE OVERVIEW, REACH, ENGAGEMENT, AUDIENCE, AND REVENUE. TO GET A THOROUGH GRASP OF YOUR AUDIENCE, LEARN HOW TO ANALYZE DATA ON VIEWS, WATCH TIME, DEMOGRAPHICS, AND OTHER TOPICS.

SETTING AND MONITORING KEY PERFORMANCE INDICATORS (KPIS)

KPIS, OR KEY PERFORMANCE INDICATORS, ARE STANDARDS USED TO GAUGE YOUR CHANNEL'S EFFECTIVENESS. START BY DEFINING MEANINGFUL KPIS THAT ARE IN LINE WITH YOUR CONTENT OBJECTIVES. DEVELOP YOUR ABILITY TO CONSISTENTLY ASSESS SUCCESS, SEE TRENDS, AND IMPROVE YOUR CONTENT STRATEGY BY LEARNING HOW TO MONITOR AND EVALUATE KPIS.

ANALYZING VIEWER RETENTION FOR CONTENT OPTIMIZATION

ONE IMPORTANT INDICATOR THAT AFFECTS HOW WELL YOUR VIDEOS PERFORM IS VIEWER RETENTION. EXAMINE METHODS FOR USING YOUTUBE ANALYTICS' AUDIENCE RETENTION DATA ANALYSIS. TO KEEP VIEWERS INTERESTED THROUGHOUT YOUR FILMS, FIND DROP-OFF AREAS, COMPREHEND AUDIENCE BEHAVIOR, AND ENHANCE YOUR MATERIAL.

UTILIZING CLICK-THROUGH RATES (CTR) FOR THUMBNAIL OPTIMIZATION

CLICK-THROUGH RATES (CTR) SHOW HOW EFFECTIVE YOUR TITLES AND THUMBNAILS ARE AT DRAWING CLICKS. INVESTIGATE THUMBNAIL OPTIMIZATION TECHNIQUES TO RAISE CTR. FIND OUT HOW TO IMPROVE YOUR MOVIES' CLICK-WORTHINESS BY USING A/B TESTING, CLEAR TITLES, AND EYE-CATCHING IMAGES.

UNDERSTANDING THE IMPORTANCE OF WATCH TIME

ONE IMPORTANT COMPONENT OF YOUTUBE'S ALGORITHM IS WATCH TIME. EXAMINE THE IMPORTANCE OF WATCH TIME AND HOW IT AFFECTS SEARCH RANKINGS AND VIDEO RECOMMENDATIONS. DISCOVER HOW TO LENGTHEN AND CAPTIVATE VIEWERS' ATTENTION WITH LONGER MATERIAL BY IMPROVING VIDEO STRUCTURES.

ANALYZING TRAFFIC SOURCES FOR STRATEGIC PROMOTION

STRATEGIC PROMOTION REQUIRES KNOWING WHERE YOUR TRAFFIC IS COMING FROM. EXAMINE THE TRAFFIC SOURCES SECTION OF YOUTUBE ANALYTICS TO LEARN MORE ABOUT HOW PEOPLE FIND YOUR CONTENT. DISCOVER HOW TO BEST UTILIZE THIS DATA TO PROMOTE YOUR BRAND BOTH ON AND OFF THE PLATFORM.

INTERPRETING AUDIENCE DEMOGRAPHICS FOR CONTENT TAILORING

THE DEMOGRAPHICS OF YOUR AUDIENCE REVEAL IMPORTANT DETAILS ABOUT THE TRAITS OF YOUR VIEWERS. EXAMINE THE AUDIENCE AREA OF YOUTUBE ANALYTICS AND DIG INTO DETAILS ABOUT AGE, GENDER, AND GEOGRAPHY. UNDERSTAND HOW TO ANALYZE DEMOGRAPHIC INFORMATION TO BETTER TARGET AND RESONATE WITH YOUR AUDIENCE WITH YOUR CONTENT.

MONITORING REVENUE AND AD PERFORMANCE

IT'S CRITICAL FOR PRODUCERS INTERESTED IN MONETIZATION TO KEEP AN EYE ON REVENUE AND AD PERFORMANCE. EXPLORE THE YOUTUBE ANALYTICS INCOME AREA TO LEARN ABOUT ANALYTICS PERTAINING TO MONETIZED PLAYBACKS, AD INCOME, AND ADSENSE. DISCOVER HOW TO ENHANCE VIEWER EXPERIENCE AND MAXIMIZE REVENUE FROM YOUR CONTENT.

LEVERAGING ADVANCED ANALYTICS TOOLS FOR DEEPER INSIGHTS

ADVANCED ANALYTICS SOLUTIONS OFFER MORE COMPREHENSIVE INSIGHTS INTO THE SUCCESS OF YOUR CHANNEL THAN YOUTUBE ANALYTICS ALONE. EXAMINE PLATFORMS AND PRODUCTS FROM THIRD PARTIES THAT PROVIDE FURTHER ANALYTICS FUNCTIONALITY. DISCOVER HOW TO UTILIZE THESE RESOURCES IN ADDITION TO YOUTUBE ANALYTICS TO GET A DEEPER GRASP OF YOUR VIEWERSHIP.

IMPLEMENTING A/B TESTING FOR CONTENT EXPERIMENTATION

CONTENT PRODUCERS CAN TRY OUT VARIOUS PARTS OF THEIR WORK BY USING A/B TESTING. EXPLORE THE IDEA OF A/B TESTING AND ITS APPLICATIONS TO CONTENT FORMATS, TITLES, THUMBNAILS, AND VIDEO STRUCTURES. DISCOVER HOW TO ADJUST YOUR CONTENT STRATEGY ACCORDING TO AUDIENCE PREFERENCES BY USING A/B TESTING.

UTILIZING DATA-DRIVEN INSIGHTS FOR CONTENT STRATEGY REFINEMENT

DATA-DRIVEN INSIGHTS ARE A USEFUL TOOL FOR FINE-TUNING YOUR CONTENT MARKETING APPROACH. EXAMINE TACTICS FOR UTILIZING ANALYTICS TO SPOT PROFITABLE CONTENT TRENDS, COMPREHEND AUDIENCE TASTES, AND MODIFY YOUR STRATEGY IN RESPONSE TO INFORMATION. DISCOVER HOW TO STRIKE A BALANCE BETWEEN DATA-DRIVEN DECISION-MAKING AND CREATIVITY FOR LONG-TERM SUCCESS.

IMPLEMENTING AUDIENCE FEEDBACK FOR ITERATIVE IMPROVEMENT

FEEDBACK FROM THE AUDIENCE IS AN IMPORTANT PART OF DATA-DRIVEN GROWTH. EXAMINE VARIOUS APPROACHES OF GATHERING AND ANALYZING VIEWER INPUT. DISCOVER HOW TO CREATE A FEELING OF COMMUNITY, ENHANCE YOUR CONTENT ITERATIVELY, AND FORTIFY YOUR RELATIONSHIP WITH YOUR AUDIENCE BY USING POLLS, COMMENTS, AND COMMUNITY INVOLVEMENT.

CONCLUSION CHAPTER 9 EMPOWERING GROWTH THROUGH INFORMED DECISIONS

REMEMBER, AS WE WRAP UP THIS CHAPTER, THAT DATA-DRIVEN STRATEGIES AND ANALYTICS ENABLE ARTISTS TO MAKE WELL-INFORMED DECISIONS, ADJUST TO AUDIENCE PREFERENCES, AND PROMOTE LONG-TERM GROWTH. YOU CAN CONFIDENTLY TRAVERSE THE DIGITAL MARKET AND KEEP IMPROVING YOUR CHANNEL FOR SUCCESS BY UTILIZING THE POWER OF DATA. CHEERS TO YOUR ANALYSIS!

CHAPTER 10
NAVIGATING YOUTUBE'S ALGORITHM

DECODING THE DIGITAL ECOSYSTEM

GREETINGS AND WELCOME TO "THE YOUTUBE LANDSCAPE UNVEILED," CHAPTER 10. THIS VIDEO DELVES INTO THE COMPLEXITIES OF YOUTUBE'S ALGORITHM, WHICH SERVES AS A DIGITAL COMPASS INFLUENCING AUDIENCE ENGAGEMENT AND CONTENT DISCOVERY. UNDERSTANDING, OPTIMIZING, AND ALIGNING YOUR CONTENT WITH THE ALGORITHMIC FORCES THAT DETERMINE THE DESTINY OF YOUR CHANNEL IS MADE EASIER WITH THE HELP OF "NAVIGATING YOUTUBE'S ALGORITHM".

UNVEILING THE CORE PRINCIPLES OF YOUTUBE'S ALGORITHM

THE FUNDAMENTAL IDEAS THAT GUIDE YOUTUBE'S ALGORITHM ARE WHAT DETERMINE WHAT MATERIAL IS RECOMMENDED. EXPLORE THESE CONCEPTS IN DETAIL, PAYING PARTICULAR ATTENTION TO WATCH DURATION, USER INVOLVEMENT, AND USER SATISFACTION. RECOGNIZE HOW THE YOUTUBE ALGORITHM GIVES MATERIAL THAT CORRESPONDS WITH VIEWER CHOICES A HIGHER PRIORITY.

CRACKING THE CODE: HOW YOUTUBE RECOMMENDS CONTENT

THE CORE OF THE YOUTUBE ALGORITHM IS THE RECOMMENDATION ENGINE. EXAMINE THE ALGORITHMS THAT UNDERLIE SEARCH RESULTS, TRENDING CONTENT, AND TAILORED RECOMMENDATIONS. DISCOVER HOW YOUTUBE USES USER BEHAVIOR ANALYSIS TO PROVIDE EACH VIEWER WITH A CUSTOMIZED VIEWING EXPERIENCE.

UNDERSTANDING THE IMPACT OF WATCH TIME ON VIDEO RANKINGS

ONE IMPORTANT FACTOR AFFECTING YOUTUBE VIDEO RANKS IS WATCH TIME. EXAMINE THE IMPORTANCE OF WATCH TIME AND HOW IT IMPACTS YOUR VIDEOS' VISIBILITY. DISCOVER HOW TO MAKE YOUR MATERIAL MORE WATCHABLE BY LEARNING ABOUT TECHNIQUES LIKE EFFICIENT PACE, CAPTIVATING STORYTELLING, AND INTERESTING INTROS.

DECIPHERING CLICK-THROUGH RATES (CTR) AND IMPRESSIONS

IMPRESSIONS AND CLICK-THROUGH RATES (CTR) ARE IMPORTANT FACTORS IN VIDEO VISIBILITY. EXAMINE HOW CTR AFFECTS HOW LIKELY IT IS THAT PEOPLE WILL RECOMMEND YOUR MOVIES. DISCOVER HOW TO IMPROVE YOUR VIDEOS' THUMBNAILS, TITLES, AND METADATA TO RAISE CTR AND MAKE THEM MORE LIKELY TO BE CLICKED.

EXPLORING THE ROLE OF USER ENGAGEMENT SIGNALS

LIKES, COMMENTS, AND SHARES ARE EXAMPLES OF USER ENGAGEMENT SIGNALS THAT OFFER INSIGHTFUL INFORMATION ABOUT HOW SATISFIED VIEWERS ARE. EXAMINE HOW RECOMMENDATIONS AND RANKS FOR VIDEOS ARE AFFECTED BY USER PARTICIPATION. FIND OUT HOW TO PROMOTE AUDIENCE PARTICIPATION AND CREATE A COMMUNITY AROUND YOUR CONTENT.

OPTIMIZING VIDEO METADATA FOR SEARCH DISCOVERABILITY

Optimizing metadata effectively is essential for search discoverability. Examine the tags, descriptions, and titles found in video metadata. Discover how to strategically add pertinent keywords and phrases to improve your films' discoverability on YouTube's search feature.

THE INFLUENCE OF SESSION WATCH TIME ON RECOMMENDATIONS

The total amount of time viewers spend on YouTube after engaging with your content is measured by session watch time. Examine how the length of the session affects how your movies are viewed by the algorithm. Discover how to make films that entice users to watch more than one in a single sitting.

CAPITALIZING ON TRENDING CONTENT AND VIRALITY

THE VISIBILITY OF YOUR CHANNEL CAN BE GREATLY IMPACTED BY VIRALITY AND TRENDING CONTENT. EXPLORE TECHNIQUES FOR PRODUCING CONTENT THAT FITS IN WITH PREVAILING TRENDS AND COULD BECOME VIRAL. DISCOVER HOW TO USE CURRENT EVENTS, ISSUES, AND CULTURAL PHENOMENA TO YOUR ADVANTAGE TO DRAW VIEWERS IN AND INCREASE THE VISIBILITY OF YOUR VIDEO.

NAVIGATING YOUTUBE'S SEARCH ALGORITHM FOR OPTIMIZATION

ONE OF THE MOST IMPORTANT FACTORS IN CONTENT DISCOVERABILITY IS YOUTUBE'S SEARCH ALGORITHM. EXAMINE THE COMPONENTS THAT AFFECT SEARCH RANKS AND THE OPERATION OF THE SEARCH ALGORITHM. DISCOVER THE BEST WAYS TO OPTIMIZE YOUR VIDEOS SO THAT THEY SHOW UP IN PERTINENT SEARCH RESULTS AND ATTRACT MORE VIEWERS TO YOUR CHANNEL.

HARNESSING THE POWER OF THUMBNAILS AND TITLES

THE INITIAL POINTS OF INTERACTION WITH POTENTIAL VIEWERS ARE TITLES AND THUMBNAILS. EXPLORE TECHNIQUES FOR CRAFTING ATTENTION-GRABBING TITLES AND THUMBNAILS THAT APPROPRIATELY CONVEY YOUR CONTENT WHILE ALSO ENCOURAGING CLICKS. DISCOVER HOW TO USE GRAPHIC COMPONENTS TO DRAW ATTENTION WHILE PRESERVING CONSISTENCY IN BRANDING.

THE IMPACT OF VIEWER SATISFACTION ON LONG-TERM SUCCESS

ONE INDICATOR THAT GOES BEYOND INDIVIDUAL VIDEOS IS VIEWER SATISFACTION. EXAMINE HOW MAINTAINING A STEADY STREAM OF HAPPY VIEWERS LEADS TO LONG-TERM SUCCESS ON YOUTUBE. DISCOVER HOW TO CREATE A DEVOTED FOLLOWING, ENCOURAGE COMMUNITY INVOLVEMENT, AND MODIFY YOUR MATERIAL IN RESPONSE TO VIEWER INPUT TO GUARANTEE CONTINUOUS ENJOYMENT.

STAYING ADAPTIVE IN A DYNAMIC ALGORITHMIC LANDSCAPE

THE YOUTUBE ALGORITHM IS DYNAMIC AND PRONE TO MODIFICATIONS. EXAMINE THE SIGNIFICANCE OF CONTINUING TO BE RESPONSIVE TO ALGORITHMIC CHANGES. DISCOVER HOW TO KEEP AN EYE ON AUDIENCE PREFERENCES, ALGORITHM UPDATES, AND INDUSTRY TRENDS TO CONSISTENTLY IMPROVE YOUR CONTENT STRATEGY FOR LONG-TERM SUCCESS.

CONCLUSION CHAPTER 10 NAVIGATING SUCCESS IN THE YOUTUBE ECOSYSTEM

AS WE COME TO THE END OF THIS CHAPTER, KEEP IN MIND THAT LEARNING HOW TO USE AND COMPREHEND YOUTUBE'S ALGORITHM IS AN ONGOING PROCESS. THROUGH ADHERENCE TO ALGORITHMIC PRINCIPLES, DISCOVERABILITY OPTIMIZATION, AND A FOCUS ON VIEWER HAPPINESS, YOU MAY EFFECTIVELY POSITION YOUR CHANNEL FOR SUCCESS WITHIN THE ALWAYS CHANGING YOUTUBE ENVIRONMENT. CHEERS TO YOUR NAVIGATION!

CHAPTER 11
ENGAGING YOUR AUDIENCE THROUGH COMMUNITY BUILDING

CULTIVATING CONNECTION IN THE DIGITAL REALM

GREETINGS AND WELCOME TO "THE YOUTUBE LANDSCAPE UNVEILED," CHAPTER 11. WE DISCUSS THE ART OF COMMUNITY BUILDING IN THIS SESSION, WHICH IS CRUCIAL FOR CREATING A LIVELY AND INTERESTED AUDIENCE. "ENGAGING YOUR AUDIENCE THROUGH COMMUNITY BUILDING" OFFERS TIPS ON HOW TO GET CLOSE TO YOUR AUDIENCE, MAKE THEM FEEL LIKE THEY BELONG, AND DEVELOP A VIBRANT COMMUNITY AROUND YOUR CONTENT.

UNDERSTANDING THE IMPORTANCE OF COMMUNITY BUILDING

BUILDING A COMMUNITY FOSTERS A FEELING OF SHARED EXPERIENCES AND CONNECTION THAT EXTENDS BEYOND VIEWERSHIP. EXPLORE THE BENEFITS OF COMMUNITY BUILDING FOR CONTENT CREATORS AND HOW IT AFFECTS AUDIENCE LOYALTY AND SUCCESS OVER THE LONG RUN.

DEFINING YOUR BRAND PERSONA AND COMMUNITY IDENTITY

ESTABLISH YOUR BRAND CHARACTER AND COMMUNITY IDENTITY PRIOR TO FORMING A COMMUNITY. EXAMINE METHODS FOR DEVELOPING A RECOGNIZABLE BRAND PERSONALITY AND IMAGE THAT APPEALS TO YOUR TARGET MARKET. TO ESTABLISH A DISTINCTIVE IDENTITY, LEARN HOW TO COMMUNICATE YOUR BELIEFS, SENSE OF STYLE, AND VOICE.

UTILIZING YOUTUBE COMMUNITY FEATURES

YOU CAN COMMUNICATE DIRECTLY WITH YOUR AUDIENCE BY USING THE COMMUNITY SERVICES THAT YOUTUBE OFFERS. EXPLORE THE DIFFERENT COMMUNITY RESOURCES, SUCH AS CHANNEL MEMBERSHIPS, POLLS, AND COMMUNITY POSTS. DISCOVER HOW TO USE THESE FEATURES TO IMPROVE COMMUNITY MEMBER ENGAGEMENT, GET FEEDBACK, AND PROVIDE THEM WITH EXCLUSIVE MATERIAL.

FOSTERING TWO-WAY COMMUNICATION WITH YOUR AUDIENCE

A VIBRANT COMMUNITY IS BUILT ON TWO-WAY COMMUNICATION. EXAMINE METHODS FOR ENCOURAGING INSIGHTFUL DIALOGUE WITH YOUR AUDIENCE. DEVELOP THE ABILITY TO REPLY TO CRITICISM, POSE INQUIRIES, AND INTERACT WITH YOUR AUDIENCE IN ORDER TO START A CONVERSATION THAT GOES BEYOND JUST YOUR VIDEOS.

ORGANIZING AND PROMOTING COMMUNITY EVENTS

EVENTS HELD IN THE COMMUNITY OFFER CHANCES FOR INTERACTION AND SHARING OF EXPERIENCES. EXPLORE PLANNING AND MARKETING COMMUNITY EVENTS, INCLUDING Q&A SESSIONS, LIVE STREAMING, AND GROUP PROJECTS. DISCOVER HOW TO BUILD EXCITEMENT, ENGAGE YOUR AUDIENCE, AND LEAVE A LASTING IMPRESSION ON YOUR COMMUNITY.

ENCOURAGING USER-GENERATED CONTENT AND CONTRIBUTIONS

GIVING YOUR AUDIENCE THE TOOLS TO PARTICIPATE IMPROVES YOUR COMMUNITY. EXAMINE TACTICS FOR PROMOTING FAN ART, COMMUNITY CONTRIBUTIONS, AND USER-GENERATED MATERIAL. DEVELOP THE ABILITY TO HIGHLIGHT AND VALUE THE INVENTIVENESS OF YOUR AUDIENCE WHILE PROMOTING A WELCOMING AND COOPERATIVE ATMOSPHERE.

CREATING A COMMUNITY CODE OF CONDUCT

CREATING A CODE OF BEHAVIOR ESTABLISHES THE FOUNDATION FOR A COURTEOUS AND UPBEAT COMMUNITY. EXAMINE THE SIGNIFICANCE OF DEVELOPING COMMUNITY NORMS THAT SUPPORT COMPASSION, INCLUSIVITY, AND POSITIVE RELATIONSHIPS. MAINTAINING A FRIENDLY WORKPLACE REQUIRES KNOWING HOW TO INTERVENE IN AND LEAD CONVERSATIONS.

RECOGNIZING AND CELEBRATING COMMUNITY ACHIEVEMENTS

REWARDING COMMUNITY ACCOMPLISHMENTS ENHANCES THE RELATIONSHIP BETWEEN THE ARTIST AND THE VIEWER. EXAMINE METHODS FOR HONORING SIGNIFICANT ANNIVERSARIES, ACHIEVEMENTS, AND COMMUNITY MEMBERS' CONTRIBUTIONS. ACQUIRE THE SKILL OF COLLECTIVE CELEBRATION TO STRENGTHEN A FEELING OF ACCOMPLISHMENT AND GRATITUDE.

UTILIZING SOCIAL MEDIA PLATFORMS FOR COMMUNITY OUTREACH

USE SOCIAL MEDIA TO EXPAND YOUR COMMUNITY OUTREACH OUTSIDE OF YOUTUBE. EXPLORE THE ADVANTAGES OF USING DISCORD, INSTAGRAM, TWITTER, AND OTHER PLATFORMS TO ENGAGE YOUR AUDIENCE. DISCOVER HOW TO EFFICIENTLY USE EACH PLATFORM TO CONNECT WITH VARIOUS COMMUNITY SEGMENTS.

BUILDING A DEDICATED COMMUNITY SPACE WITH DISCORD

DISCORD GIVES COMMUNITY MEMBERS A DEDICATED AREA TO COMMUNICATE. INVESTIGATE SETTING UP AND RUNNING A DISCORD SERVER FOR YOUR VIEWERS. WITHIN THIS DEDICATED PLACE, LEARN HOW TO HOLD DEBATES, MANAGE CHANNELS, AND CULTIVATE A SENSE OF COMMUNITY SOLIDARITY.

COLLABORATING WITH YOUR COMMUNITY ON CONTENT CREATION

ENGAGEMENT IS INCREASED WHEN COMMUNITY MEMBERS WORK TOGETHER TO CREATE CONTENT. EXPLORE METHODS FOR INCLUDING YOUR AUDIENCE IN THE PRODUCTION OF CONTENT. TO CREATE CONTENT THAT SPEAKS TO THE INTERESTS OF YOUR AUDIENCE, LEARN HOW TO ASK QUESTIONS, GATHER SUGGESTIONS, AND EVEN WORK DIRECTLY WITH THEM.

IMPLEMENTING FEEDBACK LOOPS FOR CONTINUOUS IMPROVEMENT

FEEDBACK IS AN IMPORTANT TOOL FOR ONGOING DEVELOPMENT. EXAMINE THE SIGNIFICANCE OF FEEDBACK LOOPS IN THE DEVELOPMENT OF COMMUNITIES. ACQUIRE THE SKILL OF ACTIVELY SEEKING AND USING AUDIENCE FEEDBACK TO IMPROVE YOUR MATERIAL, RESOLVE ISSUES, AND MODIFY YOUR STRATEGY IN RESPONSE TO SUGGESTIONS FROM THE COMMUNITY.

HANDLING CHALLENGES AND CONFLICT RESOLUTION

PROBLEMS CAN OCCUR IN ANY COMMUNITY. EXAMINE COPING MECHANISMS AND DISPUTE RESOLUTION TECHNIQUES. TO MAINTAIN A COURTEOUS AND UPBEAT ENVIRONMENT, LEARN HOW TO RESOLVE CONFLICTS, STEER CONVERSATIONS, AND ENFORCE COMMUNITY STANDARDS.

MEASURING COMMUNITY ENGAGEMENT AND GROWTH

ANALYZING COMMUNITY INTERACTION IS CRUCIAL TO DETERMINING THE EFFECTIVENESS OF YOUR INITIATIVES. EXAMINE MEASUREMENTS AND INDICATORS THAT SHOW THE DEVELOPMENT AND ENGAGEMENT OF THE COMMUNITY. DISCOVER HOW TO ASSESS THE HEALTH AND VIBRANCY OF YOUR COMMUNITY OVER TIME BY USING ANALYTICS TOOLS AND INSIGHTS.

CONCLUSION CHAPTER 11 NURTURING A COMMUNITY FOR LONG-TERM SUCCESS

AS WE COME TO THE END OF THIS CHAPTER, KEEP IN MIND THAT CREATING A COMMUNITY IS A CONTINUOUS EFFORT THAT CALLS FOR COMMITMENT, SINCERITY, AND A REAL CONNECTION WITH YOUR AUDIENCE. LONG-TERM SUCCESS ON YOUTUBE CAN BE ACHIEVED BY CULTIVATING A COMMUNITY THAT VALUES PLEASANT INTERACTIONS, SHARED EXPERIENCES, AND TEAMWORK. CHEERS TO CONSTRUCTING COMMUNITIES!

CHAPTER 12
OVERCOMING CHALLENGES AND BURNOUT

NAVIGATING THE PEAKS AND VALLEYS OF CONTENT CREATION

Greetings and welcome to "The YouTube Landscape Unveiled," Chapter 12. We talk about the difficulties that content creators will inevitably face and the possibility of burnout in this part. "Overcoming Challenges and Burnout" offers advice on how to identify, deal with, and lessen the obstacles that could come up in your path as a content creator.

ACKNOWLEDGING THE REALITIES OF CONTENT CREATION

There are certain difficulties associated with creating content. Examine the challenges that come with being a content creator, such as erratic motivation, outside influences, and the need to continuously produce interesting content. Recognize that overcoming obstacles is a necessary step in the creative process.

RECOGNIZING SIGNS OF BURNOUT AND MENTAL EXHAUSTION

A prevalent issue in the field of content development is burnout. Examine the symptoms of mental weariness and burnout, such as emotional depletion, creative block, and a decline in motivation. Early detection of these symptoms is essential for long-term health, so learn to spot them when you see them.

BALANCING CONSISTENCY AND QUALITY IN CONTENT CREATION

Maintaining a balance between consistency and quality is an ongoing task. Examine methods for keeping up a consistent upload schedule without sacrificing the caliber of your work. Discover how to prioritize chores, create a sustainable workflow that supports your creative vision, and set reasonable goals.

NAVIGATING EXTERNAL PRESSURES AND EXPECTATIONS

STRESS AND BURNOUT CAN BE EXACERBATED BY DEMANDS AND EXPECTATIONS FROM OUTSIDE SOURCES. EXAMINE THE EFFECTS OF OUTSIDE VARIABLES, SUCH AS PLATFORM ALGORITHMS, TRENDS, AND AUDIENCE EXPECTATIONS. DISCOVER EFFECTIVE WAYS TO HANDLE THESE DEMANDS, ESTABLISH SOUND BOUNDARIES, AND PRESERVE YOUR CREATIVE INDEPENDENCE WHILE ADJUSTING TO THE CHANGING ENVIRONMENT.

SETTING REALISTIC GOALS AND MILESTONES

REASONABLE GOAL-SETTING IS ESSENTIAL FOR SUSTAINED SUCCESS. EXAMINE THE PROCESS OF ESTABLISHING ATTAINABLE BENCHMARKS AND OBJECTIVES THAT ARE IN LINE WITH YOUR VISION. DISCOVER HOW TO CELEBRATE LITTLE ACCOMPLISHMENTS, BREAK DOWN DIFFICULT GOALS INTO MANAGEABLE ONES, AND MAINTAIN MOTIVATION WHILE TRAVELING.

ADAPTING TO ALGORITHMIC CHANGES AND TRENDS

DIGITAL PLATFORMS INHERENTLY INVOLVE ALGORITHMIC MODIFICATIONS AND DYNAMIC PATTERNS. EXAMINE TACTICS FOR REMAINING FLEXIBLE WITH YOUR CONTENT STRATEGY, KEEPING UP WITH INDUSTRY TRENDS, AND ADJUSTING TO CHANGES IN ALGORITHMS. ACKNOWLEDGE CHANGE AS A CHANCE FOR PERSONAL DEVELOPMENT RATHER THAN A BARRIER.

DEALING WITH NEGATIVE FEEDBACK AND CRITICISM

SINCE CONTENT CREATION IS PUBLIC, IT IS INEVITABLE TO GET UNFAVORABLE COMMENTS AND CRITIQUES. EXAMINE POSITIVE APPROACHES TO HANDLING CRITICISM, KEEP YOUR IDENTITY APART FROM THE MATERIAL, AND MAKE USE OF COMMENTS AS A TOOL FOR DEVELOPMENT. DISCOVER HOW TO STAY RESILIENT AND CONCENTRATE ON YOUR IMAGINATIVE VISION IN SPITE OF CRITICISM FROM OTHERS.

CULTIVATING A SUPPORTIVE CREATOR COMMUNITY

IN TRYING TIMES, A HELPFUL MAKER COMMUNITY MAY BE A GREAT ASSET. EXPLORE THE ADVANTAGES OF INTERACTING WITH OTHER CREATORS, EXCHANGING STORIES, AND PROVIDING ENCOURAGEMENT TO ONE ANOTHER. DISCOVER HOW TO CREATE A NETWORK THAT ENCOURAGES COOPERATION, INSPIRATION, AND A FEELING OF UNITY.

IMPLEMENTING SELF-CARE PRACTICES FOR WELL-BEING

MAINTAINING CREATIVITY AND WELLBEING REQUIRES SELF-CARE. EXAMINE SELF-CARE TECHNIQUES THAT PROMOTE PHYSICAL, MENTAL, AND EMOTIONAL WELL-BEING. DISCOVER HOW TO GIVE REST, RELAXATION, AND CREATIVE RECHARGING ACTIVITIES TOP PRIORITY. RECOGNIZE THAT MAINTAINING YOUR HEALTH IS ESSENTIAL TO PRODUCING MATERIAL THAT WILL LAST.

SEEKING PROFESSIONAL HELP WHEN NEEDED

GETTING PROFESSIONAL ASSISTANCE WHEN FACING DIFFICULTIES IS A SHOW OF STRENGTH. EXAMINE THE SIGNIFICANCE OF DETERMINING WHEN OUTSIDE ASSISTANCE—SUCH AS THERAPY, COUNSELING, OR MENTORSHIP—IS REQUIRED. DISCOVER HOW TO PUT YOUR MENTAL HEALTH FIRST AND GET OVER THE STIGMA ATTACHED TO ASKING FOR ASSISTANCE.

INTEGRATING BREAKS AND REST PERIODS IN YOUR SCHEDULE

ABSENCE OF PAUSES AND DOWNTIME FREQUENTLY LEADS TO BURNOUT. EXAMINE THE SIGNIFICANCE OF INCLUDING FREQUENT BREAKS IN YOUR SCHEDULE FOR CREATING CONTENT. UNDERSTAND HOW TO SET LIMITS, REALISTICALLY SCHEDULE YOUR WORK, AND SCHEDULE DOWNTIME FOR HOBBIES, LEISURE, AND NON-CONTENT GENERATING ACTIVITIES.

REKINDLING PASSION AND REDISCOVERING INSPIRATION

CREATIVE EFFORTS ARE PROPELLED BY INSPIRATION AND PASSION. EXPLORE TECHNIQUES FOR INSPIRING YOURSELF AGAIN AND IGNITING YOUR ENTHUSIASM WHEN YOU'RE FEELING BURNED OUT. DISCOVER HOW TO REKINDLE THE SPARK THAT POWERS YOUR CONTENT CREATION JOURNEY BY EXPERIMENTING WITH DIFFERENT CREATIVE CHANNELS AND TAKING ON NOVEL CHALLENGES.

CONCLUSION CHAPTER 12 EMBRACING RESILIENCE AND CONTINUAL GROWTH

AS WE GET TO THE END OF THIS CHAPTER, KEEP IN MIND THAT OVERCOMING OBSTACLES AND BURNOUT REQUIRES PERSEVERANCE AND ONGOING DEVELOPMENT. YOU MAY SUCCESSFULLY MANAGE THE HIGHS AND LOWS OF YOUR CREATIVE PATH BY ACCEPTING THE REALITY OF CONTENT PRODUCTION, PLACING A HIGH VALUE ON YOUR HEALTH, AND ADOPTING AN ADAPTABLE MENTALITY. HAVE FUN WITH YOUR CREATIONS!

CHAPTER 13
ADAPTING TO YOUTUBE'S EVOLVING POLICIES

NAVIGATING THE REGULATORY LANDSCAPE OF CONTENT CREATION

GREETINGS AND WELCOME TO "THE YOUTUBE LANDSCAPE UNVEILED," CHAPTER 13. WE EXPLORE THE EVER-CHANGING WORLD OF YOUTUBE'S RULES, STANDARDS, AND GUIDELINES IN THIS SECTION. YOUTUBE'S CONTENT RESTRICTIONS ARE CONTINUOUSLY CHANGING, AND "ADAPTING TO YOUTUBE'S EVOLVING POLICIES" OFFERS TIPS ON HOW TO COMPREHEND, ABIDE BY, AND THRIVE WITHIN ITS FRAMEWORK.

THE DYNAMIC NATURE OF CONTENT POLICIES

THE CONTENT POLICIES OF YOUTUBE ARE ALWAYS CHANGING. EXAMINE THE JUSTIFICATIONS FOR POLICY MODIFICATIONS, SUCH AS STATUTORY OBLIGATIONS, PLATFORM ADVANCEMENTS, AND USER SAFETY CONCERNS. RECOGNIZE THAT LONG-TERM SUCCESS ON THE PLATFORM DEPENDS ON YOUR ABILITY TO ADJUST TO THESE CHANGES.

STAYING INFORMED: YOUTUBE'S POLICIES AND GUIDELINES

KNOWING YOUTUBE'S RULES AND REGULATIONS IS A FUNDAMENTAL FIRST STEP TOWARD ADAPTING. EXPLORE THE MAIN FACETS OF YOUTUBE'S CONTENT POLICIES, SUCH AS THE REVENUE STRATEGIES, COMMUNITY GUIDELINES, AND COPYRIGHT LAWS. TO GUARANTEE COMPLIANCE, FIND OUT HOW TO OBTAIN THESE RULES AND CHECK THEM FREQUENTLY.

NAVIGATING COMMUNITY GUIDELINES FOR CONTENT QUALITY

YOUTUBE COMMUNITY GUIDELINES ARE THE FOUNDATION OF HIGH-QUALITY CONTENT. EXAMINE THE ELEMENTS OF COMMUNITY GUIDELINES, SUCH AS RULES AGAINST HARMFUL BEHAVIOR, CONTENT PROHIBITIONS, AND USER SAFETY. FIND OUT HOW TO MAKE YOUR CONTENT COMPLIANT WITH THESE RULES TO KEEP THE ATMOSPHERE WELCOMING AND UPBEAT.

UNDERSTANDING COPYRIGHT REGULATIONS AND FAIR USE

COPYRIGHT LAWS ARE ESSENTIAL TO THE PROCESS OF CREATING CONTENT. EXAMINE THE CONCEPTS OF FAIR USE AND COPYRIGHT AS THEY RELATE TO YOUTUBE CONTENT. DISCOVER THE BEST WAYS TO PROTECT INTELLECTUAL PROPERTY RIGHTS, MAKE APPROPRIATE USE OF CONTENT PROTECTED BY COPYRIGHT, AND STEER CLEAR OF COPYRIGHT-RELATED PROBLEMS.

ENSURING ADHERENCE TO MONETIZATION POLICIES

FOR CREATORS LOOKING FOR FINANCIAL PROSPECTS, MONETIZATION POLICIES ARE CRUCIAL. EXAMINE THE REQUIREMENTS FOR AD-FRIENDLY CONTENT, THE YOUTUBE PARTNER PROGRAM, AND THE MONETIZATION POLICIES. TO CREATE A CHANNEL THAT IS SUSTAINABLE AND OPEN UP INCOME SOURCES, LEARN HOW TO ABIDE BY THESE RULES.

ADDRESSING DEMONETIZATION AND LIMITED ADS ISSUES

LIMITED ADVERTISEMENTS AND DEMONETIZATION CAN AFFECT A CREATOR'S EARNINGS. EXAMINE FREQUENT JUSTIFICATIONS FOR DEMONETIZATION, SUCH AS ADVERTISER-FRIENDLY FACTORS AND CONTENT COMPATIBILITY. UNDERSTAND HOW TO STRIKE A BALANCE BETWEEN POLICY COMPLIANCE AND CREATIVE EXPRESSION WHILE ADDRESSING AND PREVENTING DEMONETIZATION CHALLENGES.

NAVIGATING AGE-RESTRICTED CONTENT GUIDELINES

ON YOUTUBE, CONTENT WITH AGE RESTRICTIONS NEEDS TO BE TREATED WITH EXTRA CARE. EXAMINE THE RULES ON MATURE THEMES, VIOLENCE, AND EXPLICIT LANGUAGE IN CONTENT INTENDED FOR A CERTAIN AGE GROUP. UNDERSTAND THE PROPER LABELING AND HANDLING TECHNIQUES FOR AGE-RESTRICTED CONTENT TO ABIDE BY YOUTUBE'S GUIDELINES AND SAFEGUARD YOUR VIEWERS.

MANAGING CONTROVERSIAL TOPICS AND SENSITIVE ISSUES

SENSITIVE SUBJECTS AND CONTENTIOUS TOPICS CAN PRESENT DIFFICULTIES FOR WRITERS. EXAMINE HOW TO HANDLE SUCH CONTENT WHILE ADHERING TO YOUTUBE'S RULES. LEARN HOW TO RESPECTFULLY ADDRESS DELICATE TOPICS, GIVE APPROPRIATE BACKGROUND, AND PARTICIPATE IN FRUITFUL DIALOGUES ALL WHILE ADHERING TO SOCIAL NORMS.

ADDRESSING STRIKES, WARNINGS, AND ACCOUNT PENALTIES

POLICY INFRACTIONS RESULT IN ACCOUNT FINES, WARNINGS, AND STRIKES. EXAMINE THE EFFECTS OF COPYRIGHT DISPUTES, COMMUNITY GUIDELINE STRIKES, AND OTHER SANCTIONS. DISCOVER HOW TO DEAL WITH AND CONTEST STRIKES, AS WELL AS PUT PREVENTATIVE MEASURES IN PLACE TO STOP SUCH INFRACTIONS IN THE FUTURE.

LEVERAGING TRANSPARENCY AND COMMUNICATION

ADAPTING TO POLICIES REQUIRES OPENNESS AND COMMUNICATION. EXAMINE THE SIGNIFICANCE OF KEEPING YOUR AUDIENCE INFORMED ABOUT CHANGES TO POLICIES AND CONTENT. DISCOVER HOW BEING TRANSPARENT HELPS YOU MANAGE EXPECTATIONS AND CREATE TRUST WITH YOUR AUDIENCE, WHICH WILL HELP YOU MAINTAIN A GOOD RAPPORT.

EDUCATING YOUR AUDIENCE ON POLICY COMPLIANCE

A PROACTIVE STRATEGY IS TO INSTRUCT YOUR AUDIENCE ON POLICY COMPLIANCE. LOOK AT WAYS TO NOTIFY YOUR AUDIENCE ABOUT CONTENT EXPECTATIONS, AGE RESTRICTIONS, AND COMMUNITY NORMS. DISCOVER HOW TO INVOLVE YOUR AUDIENCE IN THE CREATION OF INTERESTING CONTENT THAT COMPLIES WITH POLICIES.

COLLABORATING WITH YOUTUBE SUPPORT AND RESOURCES

YOUTUBE PROVIDES RESOURCES AND SUPPORT TO HELP ARTISTS. EXPLORE THE VARIOUS ASSISTANCE CHANNELS AT YOUR DISPOSAL, SUCH AS CREATOR INSIDER, HELP CENTER, AND CREATOR ASSISTANCE. DISCOVER HOW TO TAKE ADVANTAGE OF THESE RESOURCES FOR QUESTIONS ABOUT POLICIES, TROUBLESHOOTING, AND REMAINING CURRENT WITH PLATFORM UPDATES.

STAYING RESILIENT IN THE FACE OF POLICY CHANGES

IT IS NATURAL FOR POLICIES TO ALTER IN THE DIGITAL SPHERE. EXAMINE TACTICS FOR MAINTAINING YOUR RESILIENCE AS LAWS CHANGE. DISCOVER HOW TO MODIFY YOUR CONTENT PLAN, INTERACT WITH YOUR AUDIENCE THROUGHOUT SHIFTS, AND WELCOME CHANGE AS A CHANCE FOR DEVELOPMENT.

CONCLUSION CHAPTER 13 THRIVING AMID POLICY EVOLUTION

REMEMBER THAT ADJUSTING TO YOUTUBE'S CHANGING POLICIES IS A CONTINUOUS PROCESS AS WE COME TO THE END OF THIS CHAPTER. YOU CAN NOT ONLY ABIDE BY POLICIES BUT ALSO PROSPER AND CREATE A STRONG, LONG-LASTING YOUTUBE CHANNEL BY KEEPING EDUCATED, FOLLOWING RULES, AND ENCOURAGING OPEN DISCUSSION WITH YOUR VIEWS. CHEERS TO YOUR NAVIGATION!

CHAPTER 14
FUTURE TRENDS AND INNOVATIONS IN YOUTUBE

ANTICIPATING THE NEXT WAVE OF YOUTUBE EVOLUTION

GREETINGS AND WELCOME TO "THE YOUTUBE LANDSCAPE UNVEILED," CHAPTER 14. THIS PART FOCUSES ON THE FUTURE, EXAMINING THE DEVELOPMENTS AND TRENDS THAT ARE EXPECTED TO IMPACT YOUTUBE'S ENVIRONMENT. "FUTURE TRENDS AND INNOVATIONS IN YOUTUBE" OFFERS PERSPECTIVES ON NEW DEVELOPMENTS IN TECHNOLOGY, USER CONDUCT, AND CREATIVE OPPORTUNITIES THAT CONTENT CREATORS OUGHT TO BE READY TO SEIZE.

ANTICIPATING THE NEXT WAVE OF YOUTUBE EVOLUTION

YOUTUBE IS A LEADING FORCE IN THE RAPIDLY CHANGING DIGITAL CONTENT INDUSTRY, CONSTANTLY INFLUENCING AND CHANGING THE ONLINE VIDEO SCENE. WITH A NEW ERA APPROACHING, IT IS CRITICAL TO LOOK INTO THE CRYSTAL BALL OF USER BEHAVIOR AND TECHNOLOGY DEVELOPMENT TO FORECAST YOUTUBE'S NEXT EVOLUTION.

THE EVOLUTION OF CONTENT CONSUMPTION

THE WAY AUDIENCES CONSUME MATERIAL EVOLVES WITH TECHNOLOGY. EXAMINE NEW DEVELOPMENTS IN THE CONSUMPTION OF CONTENT, SUCH AS THE POPULARITY OF INTERACTIVE MEDIA, AUGMENTED REALITY (AR), AND VIRTUAL REALITY (VR). FIND OUT HOW TO USE THESE TECHNOLOGIES AS A CREATIVE TO INCREASE VIEWER ENGAGEMENT AND PRODUCE IMMERSIVE EXPERIENCES.

THE IMPACT OF ARTIFICIAL INTELLIGENCE ON CONTENT CREATION

CONTENT CREATION IS UNDERGOING SIGNIFICANT CHANGE AS A RESULT OF ARTIFICIAL INTELLIGENCE (AI). EXAMINE HOW AI IS USED IN CONTENT OPTIMIZATION, TAILORED RECOMMENDATIONS, AND VIDEO EDITING. DISCOVER HOW CONTENT PRODUCERS MAY USE AI TECHNOLOGIES TO IMPROVE WORKFLOWS, COMPREHEND AUDIENCE PREFERENCES, AND MAINTAIN THEIR LEADERSHIP IN CONTENT INNOVATION.

INTERACTIVE AND SHOPPABLE CONTENT EXPERIENCES

THESE DAYS, CREATING CONTENT INVOLVES A LOT OF INTERACTION. EXAMINE THE IDEA OF INTERACTIVE MEDIA, IN WHICH AUDIENCES HAVE AN ACTIVE ROLE IN THE NARRATIVE. EXPLORE THE POSSIBILITIES OF SHOPPABLE CONTENT EXPERIENCES AS WELL, WHICH ENABLE CONTENT PRODUCERS TO INCORPORATE E-COMMERCE COMPONENTS STRAIGHT INTO THEIR FILMS.

IMMERSIVE STORYTELLING WITH EXTENDED REALITY (XR)

AUGMENTED AND VIRTUAL REALITY (AR) TOGETHER FORM EXTENDED REALITY (XR), WHICH OPENS UP NEW STORYTELLING POSSIBILITIES. EXPLORE HOW XR MAY BE USED TO PRODUCE NARRATIVE EXPERIENCES THAT GO BEYOND CONVENTIONAL VIDEO FORMS. DISCOVER HOW XR CAN ENHANCE NARRATIVE AND OPEN UP NEW CREATIVE POSSIBILITIES BY IMMERSING VIEWERS IN VIRTUAL WORLDS.

IMMERSIVE STORYTELLING WITH EXTENDED REALITY (XR)

AUGMENTED AND VIRTUAL REALITY (AR) TOGETHER FORM EXTENDED REALITY (XR), WHICH OPENS UP NEW STORYTELLING POSSIBILITIES. EXPLORE HOW XR MAY BE USED TO PRODUCE NARRATIVE EXPERIENCES THAT GO BEYOND CONVENTIONAL VIDEO FORMS. DISCOVER HOW XR CAN ENHANCE NARRATIVE AND OPEN UP NEW CREATIVE POSSIBILITIES BY IMMERSING VIEWERS IN VIRTUAL WORLDS.

THE RISE OF SHORT-FORM VIDEO PLATFORMS

PLATFORMS FOR SHORT-FORM VIDEOS ARE BECOMING MORE POPULAR. CHECK OUT THE POPULARITY OF BITE-SIZED CONTENT ON SITES LIKE TIKTOK AND YOUTUBE SHORTS. DISCOVER HOW PRODUCERS CAN USE THESE CHANNELS TO THEIR ADVANTAGE TO REACH A VARIETY OF AUDIENCES AND TRY OUT CREATIVE NARRATIVE STYLES IN A SHORTER AMOUNT OF TIME.

EVOLVING TRENDS IN LIVESTREAMING AND COMMUNITY ENGAGEMENT

LIVESTREAMING IS STILL DEVELOPING AND ENCOURAGING COMMUNITY INTERACTION IN REAL TIME. EXPLORE NEW DEVELOPMENTS IN LIVESTREAMING, LIKE ONLINE CONFERENCES, Q&A SESSIONS, AND GROUP PROJECTS. DISCOVER HOW LIVESTREAMS MAY HELP PRODUCERS ESTABLISH REAL, INSTANT CONNECTIONS WITH THEIR AUDIENCE.

BLOCKCHAIN AND DECENTRALIZED CONTENT PLATFORMS

BLOCKCHAIN TECHNOLOGY IS CHANGING THE WAY THAT CONTENT IS OWNED AND DISTRIBUTED. EXAMINE THE IDEA OF DECENTRALIZED CONTENT PLATFORMS, WHICH PROVIDE CONTENT PRODUCERS MORE AUTHORITY OVER THEIR INTELLECTUAL PROPERTY AND SOURCES OF INCOME. FIND OUT HOW BLOCKCHAIN CAN EMPOWER CREATORS, LESSEN THE NEED FOR MIDDLEMEN, AND INCREASE TRANSPARENCY.

PERSONALIZATION AND AI-DRIVEN RECOMMENDATIONS

ARTIFICIAL INTELLIGENCE ALGORITHMS POWER PERSONALIZED CONTENT EXPERIENCES. EXAMINE HOW USER INTERACTIONS ON YOUTUBE ARE INFLUENCED BY AI-DRIVEN SUGGESTIONS. DISCOVER HOW CONTENT PRODUCERS MAY IMPROVE THE DISCOVERABILITY OF THEIR WORK, CUSTOMIZE SUGGESTIONS BASED ON AUDIENCE TASTES, AND PROVIDE A MORE CUSTOMIZED VIEWING EXPERIENCE.

SUSTAINABILITY AND SOCIAL RESPONSIBILITY IN CONTENT CREATION

THE VALUE OF SOCIAL RESPONSIBILITY AND SUSTAINABILITY IS RISING AMONG AUDIENCES. EXAMINE THE PART THAT ARTISTS PLAY IN ADVANCING SOCIAL JUSTICE AND ENVIRONMENTALLY SUSTAINABLE BEHAVIORS. DISCOVER THE POSITIVE EFFECTS THAT CONTENT MAY HAVE ON SOCIETY AND INVESTIGATE METHODS FOR COORDINATING ARTISTIC PURSUITS WITH SOCIAL AND ENVIRONMENTAL RESPONSIBILITIES.

EMERGING GENRES AND NICHE COMMUNITIES

ON YOUTUBE, NEW GENRES AND NICHE COMMUNITIES ARE APPEARING ALL THE TIME. EXAMINE CURRENT TRENDS IN THE PRODUCTION OF NICHE MATERIAL THAT APPEALS TO PARTICULAR HOBBIES AND SUBCULTURES. DISCOVER HOW CONTENT PRODUCERS MAY SPOT AND CAPITALIZE ON NEW GENRES TO ENGAGE FERVENT AUDIENCES AND ESTABLISH DISTINCTIVE MARKETS FOR THEIR WORK.

THE INTEGRATION OF EPHEMERAL CONTENT

WITH ITS TRANSIENT NATURE, EPHEMERAL CONTENT IS BECOMING MORE AND MORE POPULAR. EXAMINE HOW STORIES AND VANISHING MATERIAL MIGHT BE COMBINED ON YOUTUBE. DISCOVER HOW PRODUCERS CAN EXPERIMENT WITH MORE CASUAL AND IMPROMPTU STORYTELLING, GENERATE ENGAGEMENT, AND COMMUNICATE A FEELING OF URGENCY WITH EPHEMERAL MATERIAL.

DIVERSITY, INCLUSION, AND AUTHENTIC REPRESENTATION

WHEN CREATING CONTENT, DIVERSITY AND INCLUSIVITY ARE VITAL FACTORS TO TAKE INTO ACCOUNT. EXAMINE THE SIGNIFICANCE OF INCLUSIVENESS AND TRUE DEPICTION IN NARRATIVE. DISCOVER THE WAYS IN WHICH CREATORS MAY CELEBRATE DIVERSITY OF VOICE, PROMOTE POSITIVE PORTRAYAL, AND CULTIVATE AN INCLUSIVE ONLINE COMMUNITY.

CONCLUSION CHAPTER 14 EMBRACING THE UNCHARTED FUTURE OF YOUTUBE

RECALL THAT YOUTUBE HAS A BRIGHT FUTURE AHEAD OF IT, FULL OF UNKNOWNS AND THRILLING POSSIBILITIES AS WE WRAP UP THIS CHAPTER. IN THE CONSTANTLY CHANGING WORLD OF ONLINE CONTENT, PRODUCERS MAY MAINTAIN THEIR PLACE AT THE VANGUARD OF INNOVATION AND ATTRACT AUDIENCES BY REMAINING INFORMED, EMBRACING TECHNOLOGICAL IMPROVEMENTS, AND ENGAGING IN CREATIVE EXPERIMENTATION. CHEERS TO YOUR EXPLORATION!

CHAPTER 15
LEAVING A LASTING IMPACT
YOUR YOUTUBE LEGACY
CRAFTING A MEANINGFUL
LEGACY ON YOUTUBE

THIS IS THE LAST CHAPTER OF "THE YOUTUBE LANDSCAPE UNVEILED." WELCOME. IN THIS EPISODE, WE DELVE INTO THE IMPORTANT IDEA OF MAKING A LASTING IMPRESSION ON YOUTUBE. THE BOOK "LEAVING A LASTING IMPACT - YOUR YOUTUBE LEGACY" EXPLORES THE METHODS AND FRAME OF MIND NEEDED TO LEAVE A LASTING IMPACT THAT GOES BEYOND VIEWERSHIP AND SUBSCRIBERSHIP.

DEFINING YOUR CREATIVE VISION AND PURPOSE

A DISTINCT CREATIVE VISION AND PURPOSE ARE NECESSARY FOR CREATING AN EFFECT THAT LASTS. EXAMINE THE SIGNIFICANCE OF OUTLINING YOUR GOALS, PRINCIPLES, AND THE KIND OF IMPACT YOU HOPE TO ACHIEVE WITH YOUR WRITING. DISCOVER HOW YOU MAY CONNECT MORE DEEPLY WITH AUDIENCES BY DIRECTING YOUR CREATIVE EFFORTS TOWARD A HIGHER GOAL.

BUILDING AUTHENTIC CONNECTIONS WITH YOUR AUDIENCE

A SIGNIFICANT LEGACY IS BUILT ON GENUINE TIES. EXPLORE TECHNIQUES FOR DEVELOPING SINCERE CONNECTIONS WITH YOUR AUDIENCE. DEVELOP YOUR ABILITY TO INTERACT WITH YOUR AUDIENCE, ANSWER THEIR FEEDBACK, AND CREATE A COMMUNITY THAT EXISTS OUTSIDE OF THE SCREEN. BEING GENUINE FORGES A STRONG CONNECTION WITH YOUR AUDIENCE.

CONTRIBUTING POSITIVELY TO ONLINE COMMUNITIES

POSITIVE EFFECTS ARE SEEN BY THE LARGER ONLINE COMMUNITY IN ADDITION TO YOUR CHANNEL. LOOK FOR WAYS TO ASSIST OTHER CREATORS, HAVE PRODUCTIVE INTERACTIONS, AND MAKE POSITIVE CONTRIBUTIONS TO ONLINE SPACES. FIND OUT HOW YOU CAN USE YOUR INFLUENCE TO CREATE A LIVELY, INCLUSIVE, AND SUPPORTIVE ONLINE COMMUNITY.

EMBRACING YOUR EVOLUTION AS A CREATOR

FOR A CREATION TO HAVE A LASTING INFLUENCE, ONE MUST ACCEPT THAT CREATORS GROW. EXPLORE THE IDEA OF CREATIVE EVOLUTION BY TRYING OUT DIFFERENT FORMS AND MODIFYING YOUR WORK IN RESPONSE TO COMMENTS FROM YOUR AUDIENCE. FIND OUT HOW ACCEPTING CHANGE PROMOTES RELEVANCE OVER THE LONG RUN AND CONSISTENT PARTICIPATION.

DOCUMENTING MILESTONES AND CELEBRATING ACHIEVEMENTS

MARKING YOUR PROGRESS WITH DOCUMENTS IS ONE APPROACH TO HONOR YOUR JOURNEY. DISCUSS WITH YOUR AUDIENCE THE SIGNIFICANCE OF ACKNOWLEDGING AND APPRECIATING ACCOMPLISHMENTS OF ALL SIZES. DISCOVER HOW SHARING YOUR ACHIEVEMENT WITH OTHERS MAKES YOU FEEL ACCOMPLISHED AND LETS THEM EXPERIENCE YOUR SUCCESS WITH YOU.

FOSTERING A POSITIVE AND INCLUSIVE COMMUNITY

A COMMUNITY THAT IS WELCOMING AND UPBEAT IS A SIGN OF A LEGACY THAT LASTS. EXAMINE HOW MAKERS CAN HELP TO CREATE AN ENVIRONMENT WHERE EVERYONE IS WELCOME AND VARIOUS OPINIONS ARE HEARD. DISCOVER HOW TO RESOLVE DISPUTES, ESTABLISH GROUND RULES FOR THE COMMUNITY, AND MAKE SURE YOUR CHANNEL IS A WELCOMING AND SAFE PLACE.

EDUCATING AND INSPIRING THROUGH YOUR CONTENT

FOR SPECTATORS, MOTIVATION AND EDUCATION LEAVE A LASTING IMPRESSION. EXAMINE TECHNIQUES FOR PRODUCING CONTENT THAT INSPIRES, INFORMS, AND AMUSES YOUR AUDIENCE. DISCOVER HOW TO IMPART KNOWLEDGE, TELL POIGNANT TALES, AND MAKE AN IMPACT THAT LASTS LONGER THAN A VIDEO.

GIVING BACK AND SOCIAL RESPONSIBILITY

ARTISTS HAVE THE ABILITY TO UPHOLD SOCIETAL RESPONSIBILITY AND GIVE BACK. EXPLORE THE IDEA OF LEVERAGING YOUR PLATFORM FOR SOCIAL GOOD, WHETHER IT IS THROUGH CAMPAIGNS FOR AWARENESS, CHARITY GIVING, OR ASSISTANCE WITH SOCIAL CAUSES. FIND OUT HOW YOU CAN POSITIVELY IMPACT SOCIETY WITH YOUR INFLUENCE.

EMPOWERING OTHERS TO FIND THEIR VOICE

TO LEAVE A LASTING LEGACY, ONE MUST ENABLE PEOPLE TO SPEAK FOR THEMSELVES. LOOK INTO OPPORTUNITIES TO MENTOR, ASSIST UPCOMING ARTISTS, AND IMPART KNOWLEDGE GAINED FROM YOUR EXPERIENCE. FIND OUT HOW GUIDING PEOPLE THROUGH THE DIFFICULTIES OF CREATING CONTENT LEAVES A LEGACY THAT GOES BEYOND PERSONAL ACHIEVEMENT.

PRESERVING YOUR CONTENT FOR FUTURE GENERATIONS

MAINTAINING YOUR CONTENT WILL GUARANTEE THAT IT HAS AN INFLUENCE ON FUTURE GENERATIONS. EXAMINE THE SIGNIFICANCE OF KEEPING UP WITH, ORGANIZING, AND PRESERVING YOUR BODY OF WORK. FIND OUT HOW YOUR WORK CAN SERVE AS A TIME CAPSULE THAT WILL REVEAL DETAILS ABOUT YOUR CREATIVE PROCESS YEARS DOWN THE ROAD.

CONTINUAL ADAPTATION TO TECHNOLOGICAL ADVANCES

THE FIELD OF CONTENT GENERATION IS SHAPED BY TECHNOLOGICAL ADVANCEMENTS. EXAMINE THE SIGNIFICANCE OF CONTINUOUSLY ADJUSTING TO NEW TECHNOLOGIES. DISCOVER HOW KEEPING UP WITH ADVANCEMENTS AND TRENDS HELPS YOU STAY CURRENT AND USE NEW TOOLS TO IMPROVE YOUR CREATIVE EXPRESSION.

REFLECTING ON YOUR JOURNEY AND EVOLUTION

For artists, reflection is a very useful tool. Examine the significance of taking stock of your path, recognizing your progress, and drawing lessons from events. Discover the benefits of self-reflection for personal growth, artistic development, and the continuous creation of a lasting legacy.

PASSING ON WISDOM TO FUTURE CREATORS

Future creators receive a gift when we impart wisdom. Examine the idea of mentoring, exchanging thoughts, and adding to the creator community's collective knowledge. Find out how you can mentor and motivate the upcoming generation of content creators with your experiences.

CONCLUSION CHAPTER 15
THE TIMELESS IMPACT OF YOUR CREATIVE JOURNEY

AS WE GET TO THE END OF THIS CHAPTER AND "THE YOUTUBE LANDSCAPE UNVEILED," KEEP IN MIND THAT YOUR YOUTUBE CREATIVE JOURNEY HAS THE POWER TO MAKE A LASTING IMPRESSION. YOU MAY CREATE A LASTING LEGACY THAT CONNECTS WITH AUDIENCES AND GOES BEYOND THE DIGITAL SPHERE BY ENCOURAGING AUTHENTICITY, MAKING MEANINGFUL RELATIONSHIPS, AND WORKING FOR THE GREATER GOOD. CHEERS TO YOUR CREATIVE LEGACY'S LONG-LASTING IMPACT AND HAPPY CRAFTING!

DEAR READERS,

AS YOU COME TO THE END OF "YOUTUBE MASTERY 2024: UNVEILING THE SECRETS OF CONTENT CREATION," I WOULD LIKE TO EXPRESS MY SINCERE GRATITUDE FOR BEING A PART OF THIS FASCINATING EXPLORATION OF THE EVER CHANGING YOUTUBE LANDSCAPE.

YOUR DEDICATION TO PERFECTING THE ART OF YOUTUBE IS ADMIRABLE IN THE WORLD OF ONLINE VIDEO CREATION, WHERE ADVANCEMENTS CONSTANTLY REDEFINE THE LANDSCAPE AND TRENDS CHANGE LIKE THE WIND. THE KNOWLEDGE AND IDEAS IN THIS BOOK ARE INTENDED TO INSPIRE AND ENCOURAGE YOU, WHETHER YOU ARE AN EXPERIENCED CREATOR OR ARE JUST STARTING OUT, AND TO HELP YOU NAVIGATE THE COMPLEXITIES OF THE YOUTUBE WORLD.

RECALL THAT GENUINE STORYTELLING, ESTABLISHING CONNECTIONS, AND MAKING AN IMPRESSION ARE THE MAIN GOALS OF YOUTUBE MASTERY RATHER THAN FOCUSING SOLELY ON ALGORITHMS, KEYWORDS, OR TRENDS. ACCEPT THE CHANGES, DON'T STRAY FROM YOUR ARTISTIC VISION, AND ALLOW THE HUGE DIGITAL SPACE TO HEAR YOUR DISTINCT VOICE.

I HOPE THAT AS YOU START YOUR YOUTUBE CAREER, EVERY VIDEO WILL SERVE AS A CANVAS FOR YOUR CREATIVITY, EVERY SUBSCRIBER WILL ATTEST TO YOUR INFLUENCE, AND EVERY OBSTACLE WILL PRESENT A CHANCE FOR IMPROVEMENT. I THINK YOUR TALE HAS THE ABILITY TO INSPIRE OTHERS, AND YOUR MASTERY OF YOUTUBE IS A JOURNEY RATHER THAN A DESTINATION.

I APPRECIATE YOU LETTING ME BE YOUR GUIDE DURING THIS INVESTIGATION. CHEERS TO YOUR PROSPERITY, INVENTIVENESS, AND THE LASTING IMPRESSION YOU WILL UNDOUBTEDLY MAKE ON THE VIVID CANVAS OF YOUTUBE.

HAPPY CREATING!

[R.H RIZVI]

BOOK CONCLUSION

"YOU'VE BEEN TAKEN ON A THOROUGH EXPLORATION OF THE COMPLEX WORLD OF YOUTUBE VIDEO CREATION BY "THE YOUTUBE MASTERY." EVERY CHAPTER WAS DESIGNED TO EQUIP YOU WITH KNOWLEDGE AND INSIGHTS, COVERING TOPICS SUCH AS COMPREHENDING THE PLATFORM'S DYNAMICS, ADJUSTING TO CHANGING POLICIES, INVESTIGATING FUTURE TRENDS, AND LEAVING A LASTING IMPACT.

WHEN YOU START YOUR OWN YOUTUBE VENTURES, KEEP IN MIND THAT SUCCESS IS DETERMINED BY MORE THAN JUST VIEWS OR SUBSCRIBERS—IT'S ALSO ABOUT THE DEEP RELATIONSHIPS YOU BUILD, THE GOOD THINGS YOU DO, AND THE LEGACY YOU LEAVE BEHIND. AS A CREATOR, STAY TRUE TO YOURSELF, WELCOME CHANGE, AND KEEP GROWING BECAUSE YOU KNOW THAT YOUR DISTINCT VOICE WILL INSPIRE AND CONNECT WITH PEOPLE FOR A VERY LONG TIME.

WE APPRECIATE YOUR PARTICIPATION IN THIS YOUTUBE EXAMINATION OF COMMUNITY, CREATIVITY, AND INNOVATION. I HOPE YOUR TRIP IS FULL OF IMAGINATION, TENACITY, AND THE SATISFACTION OF MAKING A LASTING IMPRESSION ON THE DYNAMIC FIELD OF ONLINE CONTENT CREATION. HAVE FUN WITH YOUR CREATIONS!

www.ingramcontent.com/pod-product-compliance
Lightning Source LLC
Chambersburg PA
CBHW071050290526
45795CB00004B/1418